ARE WE STILL GRADING STUDENTS?

Are We Still Grading Students?

MARK SKELDING

ONION
RIVER
PRESS

Burlington, Vermont

Onion River Press
191 Bank Street
Burlington, VT 05401

ISBN 978-1-949066-74-6

To my good-hearted and sweet-spirited children, Sam and Sarah, and to my wife and best friend, Linda, whose progressive leadership in curriculum, assessment, and instruction is and always has been way ahead of the times.

CONTENTS

Foreword

Nothing is static; everything is in a constant state of evolution. This is one principle on which critical social theory is based and it applies to the theory itself. Although the theory has diversified into numerous offshoots since its emergence its original essence has remained consistent. It calls on us to be continually reflecting on and critiquing how fair, equitable, and inclusive our social constructs are, and whether or not we and our social constructs are allowing every individual equal freedom and opportunity to succeed and meet their full potential. Is there a social construct any more important to be looking at through a critical social lens than education?

There are many theories, orientations, and traditions related to critical social theory, all of which fall under the general umbrella of progressive thought. They include living systems theory, ecology, social ecology, social justice, phenomenology, hermeneutics, transformation theory, process theory, chaos-complexity theory, social learning theory, experiential theory, and constructivist theory to name several. The common theme inherent in progressive thought is the understanding that everything is in a constant state of progressive change fueled by formative feedback processes. My work on grading, which I share with you in this book, was grounded in constructivism, ecology, social justice, phenomenology, and systems theory.

My writing on the topic of grading began in 1995 and carried through to 2013. I have deliberately not revised or updated any of these written pieces because my intent in sharing them in their original form is to both contribute to the continuing discussion about grading (see Blum(Ed.), 2020 for example) and to allow the reader to compare then with now.

Back then we had constructivist learning theory, differentiated instruction, No Child Left Behind, performance-based assessment, state standards, Common Core Standards and Grade Level Expectations, backwards design, formative assessment, rubrics, portfolios, and standards-based report cards.

Today we have constructivist learning theory, differentiated instruction, Common Core, Next Generation Science, and C-3 Social Studies Standards, universal design, flexible pathways, profile of a graduate, personalized learning, proficiency-based learning, transferrable skills, targets and scales, proficiency indicators, and student voice and agency.

Things appear to be different now compared to ten and twenty years ago. *But is the way we now measure and report student learning truly different from back then?* My hope is that the writings contained in this book will help readers determine whether the old adage of "the more things change, the more they stay the same" applies to grading.

Admittedly, Sections One and Two are "dry" reading. However, the background information in each section is vital to any discussion on grading.

Readers will find some redundancy between certain writings. I have chosen to leave the redundancy as is because 1) for comparative purposes between then and now it's important the original text of each piece not be compromised, and 2) to highlight the need all of us had at the time for repeated exposure to information that was causing us tremendous cognitive dissonance and greatly perturbing our paradigms.

~ I ~

ASSESSMENT

Proposition
Every single interaction we have with a student is a potential opportunity for assessment. This is not the case with evaluation (grading).

Formative Assessment
Formative assessment is the process of continually monitoring and measuring learning as it emerges and develops (*"forms"*), while at the same time continually gathering feedback and responding to that feedback in a way that shapes (*"forms"*) both the learner's subsequent learning and the teacher's subsequent instruction. It is a never ending cycle in which teaching and learning both shape and are shaped by one another.

Assessment
The term assessment comes from the root word *assidere*, which means to sit beside and assist. (Herman, et.al., 1992)

Assessment is the ongoing gathering and documentation of information for the sole purpose of monitoring and following the growth of student learning. It is a deliberate process by which all parties involved continually observe and reflect on how well students are progressing toward desired goals, specific outcomes, and eventually attaining local, state, and national standards.

Assessment is the process of working alongside students, monitoring their progress and providing ongoing feedback as they construct meaning, uncover mysteries, and perpetuate their innate curiosity. It is purposeful, informative (i.e., provides meaningful feedback), influences lesson planning, directs subsequent instruction, prepares students to perform well when it comes time for evaluation, and ultimately assists students in attaining academic standards.

Assessment is a qualitative process of guiding students as they progress. And finally, assessment is formative (i.e., it continually evolves as it co-evolves with instruction; it shapes and in turn is shaped by instruction and the assessment that accompanies that instruction).

Assessment and Assessments

Assessment is the process of continually soliciting demonstration from students as a way to gather information, collect data, analyze evidence, and monitor and measure progress.

Assessments are the items we use when we are conducting assessment.

Implied in the definition of assessment and inherent in the process of assessment are 1) ongoing documentation (i.e., maintaining student classroom formative assessment portfolios) and 2) providing students with multiple opportunities to make continuous progress.

Types of Formative Assessments

Tools: Formal rubrics and checklists with spelled-out criteria against which a student's performance is compared/measured

↓ ↑

Products: Concrete, student-generated creations that directly reflect the knowledge, skills, and criteria the student has attained, with documentation of that learning being the products themselves, artifacts of the products, or photographs of the products (e.g., written pieces, models, dioramas, drawings, projects, diagrams)

Performances : Authentic documentations of the actual skills and criteria in which students are being assessed, documented through anecdotal records, photographs, or audio/video tape (e.g., simulations, role playing, problem solving, research, investigations)

Tasks: Teacher created check-in exercises which students are asked to complete as a way of providing information regarding their learning (e.g., surveys, journal entries, questionnaires, worksheets, ungraded quizzes and tests, and graphic organizers such as Venn diagrams and concept webs)

Anecdotes: Relatively informal (mental notes, jotted notes) or more formal (field notes, anecdotal observation logs) records of observed student progress/performance

Note: The two arrows between tools and the other four general types of assessments symbolize the cyclical nature of instruction and assessment. The tools (rubrics/checklists), which list the criteria of our standards, drive the design and implementation of the day-to-day standards-based enabling activities (tasks, products, performances) we provide our students. The student work that results from those activities is then measured back up against those rubrics and/or checklists, which in turn drives the design and implementation of subsequent enabling activities for our students, and so on and so on.

Things to Think About as You Plan and Design Your Multi-faceted Assessment Activities

Multi-faceted assessment is assessment that utilizes multiple means (tasks, products, performances, built-in anecdotal observation opportunities, tools) to gather evidence on student progress. Children in our classrooms possess a diversity of learning styles and employ a variety of different intelligences as they construct knowledge. If children learn differently, it follows that children best express what they know in different ways as well. This is just one reason why it is so important *to use a variety of different means* when instructing and assessing students.

It's not what it is that determines whether it's a task, product, performance, or anecdotal observation, it's what you're using it for to assess that determines what type it is. For example, a diorama is a *product* if you're using it to assess the student's reading comprehension. It's a tangible piece of evidence that reflects what the student comprehended. But if you are using that diorama to assess the student's diorama making skills then it would be a *performance* because they are actually doing (performing) the skill you're actually assessing. A KWL (what I Know, what I Want to know, what I've Learned) graphic organizer would be a *task* if you're using it to assess a student's level of knowledge and it would be a *performance* if you're using it to assess their skill at filling out a KWL.

There can be cases where a single assessment activity qualifies as more than one of the five types. For example, a class presentation can be a *product* (something the student has produced) but also a *performance* if you're using that presentation to assess their growth in the speaking standard.

Five Levels of Assessment

At what level of criteria are we assessing students? Knowing for sure that we are actually assessing the students in the actual criteria of the standards is critical. If we are assessing students in criteria other than those of the standards then we are assessing them at some level other than the generalized-standard level.

Task-specific Criteria

If we are assessing students in criteria specific to the task the students are being asked to complete (for example, journals and journaling ... criteria specific to what the journal should include or criteria specific to how to keep a journal) we are doing task-specific assessment.

Content-specific Criteria

If we are assessing students in criteria specific to the specific facts that comprise the content being taught (for example, if the content is local environment a content-specific criterion might be to name and identify ten species of native trees) we are doing content-specific assessment.

Teacher-specific Criteria

If we are assessing students in criteria specific to an individual teacher's personal expectations (for example, putting your full name and date in the top right hand corner) we are doing teacher-specific assessment.

Generalized Criteria

If we are assessing students in criteria that are so general they cut across subject areas and/or grade levels, but are not criteria embedded in the academic standards teachers and students are accountable for teaching and learning respectively (for example, loving to learn, thinking ecologically, survival skills ... these are all generalized but none of these are standards in our Vermont Framework) we are doing generalized assessment.

Generalized-standard Criteria

If we are assessing students in criteria that are actually embedded in the language of the actual academic standards teachers and students are accountable for teaching and learning respectively (for example, understanding the concept of prejudice and understanding its effects on various groups {VT Standard 4.4}) we are doing generalized-standard assessment.

Why Put Time and Effort Into Understanding the Different Types and Levels of Assessment?

Reviewing the five different types of assessments (tasks, products, performances, built-in anecdotal observation opportunities, and tools) reminds us of the importance of:

Accommodating varying learning styles ... Children learn best in different ways, therefore it follows that children are able to best express what they know in different ways. Not everyone can best express what they truly know and understand by way of just tasks (e.g., paper and pencil tests), for example.

Triangulation ... "Uni-faceted" assessment (i.e., using just one type of assessment) is not a reliable approach to gathering valid data. No single type of assessment can ever comprehensively reflect the complexity of one's knowledge and understanding. By combining information gathered through multiple means of assessment (also known as *multi-faceted assessment*) we are more likely to obtain a more valid assessment of what a child truly knows, understands, and can do.

Reviewing the five levels of assessment (task-specific, content-specific, teacher-specific, generalized, and generalized-standard) reminds us of the importance of:

Criteria-based assessment ... Knowing ahead of time what the criteria are that we are assessing students in is essential. Knowing exactly what it is we're looking for and ensuring that the enabling (formative assessment) activities that we develop are, in fact, giving us that particular information is critical.

Generalized-standard assessment ... If nothing else, at a minimum we are obligated to be assessing students in the actual criteria of the actual Vermont Standards, and measuring on an ongoing basis their progress toward "attaining" those standards. Knowing exactly how assessment at the generalized-standard level looks compared to assessment at those other four levels is critical.

Multi-Faceted, Multi-Dimensional, and Inclusive Assessment

Multi-faceted assessment is assessment that utilizes multiple means to gather evidence on student progress. Children in our classrooms possess a diversity of learning styles and employ a variety of different intelligences as they construct knowledge. If children learn differently, it follows that children best express what they know in different ways as well. This is just one reason why it is so important *to use a variety of different means* when instructing and assessing students.

A second realm of assessment important to address is *multi-dimensional assessment*. This is assessment used to check in on the student on many different levels. Holistic and brain-based learning theories explain that learning is the result of a complex interplay between the *cognitive, social, emotional, physical, and moral/spiritual domains*. A simple example ... educators have long known that if a child is not emotionally available for learning, any attempt to measure cognition during that time generally will not yield a true picture of what the child knows and understands. If students are assessed in only one domain, which in schools is typically the cognitive domain, those results are an incomplete picture of the child's true knowledge and understanding. A second example of multi-dimensional, although domain specific, is what occurs when one purposefully assesses students at every level in Bloom's Taxonomy, a scale of higher order thinking skills delineated by Benjamin Bloom that begins with simple recall of facts and ascends to skills such as being able to apply knowledge and synthesize divergent bits of information into new knowledge.

The third realm of assessment is *inclusive* assessment. Inclusive assessment incorporates as many different perspectives from as many different stakeholders as possible. This is especially critical given what phenomenology and ethnographic research say regarding subjectivity and the importance of factoring in perspective. Inclusive assessment at the classroom level can include the *teacher, student, peers, and parents*. Including community members in the process provides a particularly valuable "outside" reliability check.

Multi-Dimensional Assessment

Every classroom teacher formatively assesses their students' *cognitive* development. Most classroom teachers also formatively assess their students' *social* development.

Typically, the physical education and health teachers are the ones who formatively assess the students' *physical* development.

But who is formatively assessing the students' *moral/spiritual/ ethical* and *emotional* development?

The irony in this is that if forced to have to identify which of the five domains most influences a child's cognitive and social development we would probably pick these two domains that we formatively teach and assess the least.

Whether or not these two domains are actually being formally and formatively assessed, at a minimum we need to:

- Acknowledge that they influence learning
- Deliberately create opportunities that will draw them out (help get us in touch with our students at these levels)
- Recognize when they are impacting a student's learning
- Respond to that impact accordingly (with individualized, differentiated instruction)

In other words, at a minimum we need to be purposeful, reflective, and responsive.

Classroom Formative Assessment

1. Practice Backwards Design (Wiggins & McTighe, 1998)
   Focus first on the power standards (see Section Five) and general criteria embedded in those standards.

2. Create Power Standards Progress Rubrics
   Develop progress rubrics (or checklists if more appropriate) that list the criteria and their respective benchmarks of growth for each standard being worked on.

3. Work *From* Your Power Standards Progress Rubrics
   Let the criteria of the standards guide your planning and drive your instruction.

4. Purposefully Design Daily Enabling Activities (Assessment Activities)
   Provide a multi-faceted mix of standards-based tasks, products, performances, and built-in anecdotal observation opportunities that allow for simultaneous instruction and assessment and allow students multiple opportunities to increase their proficiency in the criteria of the power standards.

5. Maintain Classroom Formative Assessment Portfolios
   Collect student work (completed tasks, products, performance artifacts), tools (rubrics/checklists), and anecdotal records and keep it all in portfolios that are accessible for both student and teachers to work from and toward.

6. Work *Toward* Your Power Standards Progress Rubrics
   On an ongoing basis, as collaboratively (inclusively) as possible, monitor and measure student progress up against the benchmarks on these tools.

7. Purposefully Design Daily Enabling Activities (Assessment Activities)
   Use ongoing assessment results to drive your subsequent multi-faceted rounds of standards-based tasks, products, per-

formances, and built-in anecdotal opportunities that allow students additional multiple opportunities to increase their proficiency in the criteria of the power standards.

8. Repeat Steps 3 Through 7 Indefinitely
9. Periodically Report Progress
10. Provide feedback for all stakeholders involved on how well students are progressing in the criteria of the power standards.

Classroom Formative Assessment Portfolios

A classroom formative assessment portfolio is a student's accumulating body of work that reflects the student's learning. It's maintained over time and it is a "working" portfolio.

It contains a triangulated, multi-faceted mix of tasks, products, performance artifacts, tools (rubrics, checklists), and anecdotal observation records that all serve as evidence of the student's growth in the standards.

And the fact that it is a "working" portfolio means it is accessible to both the teacher and student to continually refer to see at a glance not just where the student was and where she is now, but what the work contained within suggests are next steps to keep moving her forward. In other words it doesn't just contain all of the student's formative assessments, it, itself, is a formative assessment.

Whether hard copy or electronic a classroom formative assessment portfolio is as much a concept/process/practice as it is a thing.

~ II ~

EVALUATION (GRADING)

Evaluation

The term evaluation comes from the root words *valu*, which means to judge, determine a worth for, place a value on, appraise, and grade, and *valere*, which means strength. (Herman, et.al., 1992) Evaluation is a process used to attempt to capture and define something's worth by comparatively categorizing it and then assigning it a *fixed* (emphasis intentional, see Section Three) value.

Summative Evaluation

Summative evaluation is the practice of periodically attempting to sum, rank, and then assign value to the learner's overall ability at a given point in time. In other words, evaluation is the process of *grading* a student's competency or the worth of his work. It is a *final* (emphasis intentional, See Section Three) judgment of a student's performance or ability. Unlike assessment (measuring growth), evaluation (grading) is strictly a summative process. Evaluation, summative evaluation, and grading are all synonymous.

As we can see, assessment and evaluation (grading) are in no way synonymous and are not terms that can or should be used interchangeably. In fact the two practices are antithetical.

13

Key Terms

Three key terms important to distinguish are measurement, scoring, and grading. *Measurement* is the process of comparing a student's performance up against explicit benchmarks (performance targets). The way in which rubrics are used as formative assessment tools is an example of measurement.

Scoring is the practice of using a number to report a student's level of achievement relative to a particular number of criteria. For example, a score of getting 80 correct out 100 is 80/100 or 80%. A second example is if a student makes progress in 3 out 4 of a standard's criteria the student's score would be 3/4 or 75%.

Grading is the practice of using a letter, number, proficiency label, or symbol to summarily categorize and assign worth to a student's degree of proficiency within a cut-score grading scale. For example, if we take the above student's 80% and equate that to a B or if we take the other student's 3 out of 4 and equate that to a "3" or "Meets the Standard" then we have engaged in grading.

Grades

Evaluation naturally involves assigning grades (grading). Grading is evaluation. Anytime a cut-score scale is used to sort, rank, compare, categorize, and place relative worth on a student's performance grading is occurring.

Grades and their accompanying cut-score grading scales come in all forms. Some common examples include:

Letter grades such as A-B-C-D-F and P (Pass)-F (Fail)

Number grades such as the 1-2-3-4 system commonly used with report cards that are commonly called "standards-based" report cards.

Proficiency labels such as Good Start-Almost There- Got It-Wow; Introducing-Below Standard-Meets Standard-Beyond Standard; Beginning-Progressing-Proficient-Exceptional; Poor-Fair-Good-Excellent; Unsatisfactory-Satisfactory-Outstanding

Symbols such as a Sad Face-Neutral Face-Smiley Face

Cut-Score Grading Scales

There are pre-determined and post-determined (derived after the students' scores are in) cut-score grading scales. Within these two categories we find a variety of different cut-score scales being used by teachers.

1. The fixed traditional 100-90=A, 89-80=B, etc. one scale fits all scale
2. The adjusted scale ... when a significant number of scores come in low, scores that would have been judged to be worth a C on the traditional scale are now judged to be worth an A and then the rest of the grades are assigned from there.
3. The "normal distribution (bell)" curve where pre-set percentages of students are allowed to land in each of the grade categories on the scale.
4. The natural gap scale in which the teacher lists all the scores in order from highest to lowest and where there's a significant gap between two scores that gap becomes the line drawn between one grade and the next.
5. The differentiated scales (ex. something with just 8 items might have a scale of 6-8=A, 4-5=B, 3=C, 2=D, 0-1=F) ... often just an equivalent to the 90-80-70 etc. scale.
6. The 5-4-3-2-1-0 scale now being used in response to no longer giving unfair zeros within the traditional 100-90-80 etc. scale.
7. The rating scales such as Excellent-Satisfactory-Fair-Poor.
8. The 4-3-2-1 or Beyond Standard-At Standard-Below Standard-Introduced scales, commonly referred to as standards-based grading scales.*

*Simply using these particular grading scales and ensuring our report card lists the standards are not what qualifies our report card as "standards-based." Whether it's a standards-based report card or not depends on whether continuous standards-based formative instruction and assessment aligning with that report card is occurring in the classroom. In other words if the standards are the primary focus of what's being taught, the students are continually being assessed on their growth in the actual criteria of those standards using standards-based progress rubrics (see Section Five), and the grades that end up on the report card are valid reflections of the students' actual growth in those standards as evidenced by all the standards-based formative assessments that have been steadily collected on the student, then we can rest assured our report card is actually a standards-based report card.

Is That an Assessment or an Evaluation?

It's not what it is that determines whether it's an assessment or an evaluation, it's how it's used. For example, if a traditional test or quiz is corrected (ex. the student gets 88 correct out of 100 {88/100}) and then that score (+88) is inserted into a cut-score grading scale (ex. 80-89=B) and converted into a grade (ex. B+), then it's an evaluation. But if it is simply corrected, scored (ex. +88 or 88/100), and then used to provide feedback for the student on how to increase her learning of that topic in preparation for the next time her growth in her learning of that topic is checked in on (assessed) then it's assessment.

Some Overarching Questions

- Is grading, and the way in which we derive and use grades, complementing and promoting what our school's mission statement says about who we are as a school and what we believe about children and learning?
- What evidence do we have that grades are any more or less motivating than scores? In other words, why would a student who got a C but wants an A be any less motivated than if she got 2 out of 5 but wants 5 out of 5?

- What *if* every student gets an A? Why is that a problem? Shouldn't that be cause for celebration?
- Why give grades as opposed to scores or measurements?
- Why average the students' grades rather than simply reporting sums?
- Why grade the students' scores rather than simply reporting the scores themselves?

An Issue with Averaging: A Spelling Example

With either of the following two approaches to teaching a flaw with averaging is evident.

Approach number one is the traditional scope-and-sequence style where the student gets a new set of words each week and is tested on those words at week's end. If the student gets 6 out of 20 words correct on test one, 12 out of 20 on test two, and 18 out of 20 on test three her average would be 12. However, the number of words she appears to know how to spell at the time of reporting is actually 36, not 12.

Approach number two is the standards-based style where the student is allowed to work on internalizing a set of words over time and across contexts. Using the same test scores as above the student has demonstrated at reporting time that she knows how to spell 18 words, not 12.

Issues with Averaging: Example Two

Angel's grades listed in the Social Studies Grade Book – Marking Period 1 are:

Unit test 1=**B-**; Unit test 2=**C-**; Unit test 3=**A**; Homework=**B+**; Participation=**A+**

His overall average is a B+. What does Angel's B+ for Marking Period One tell us about what he actually knows and is able to do with regard to Social Studies at that moment in time?

Weighting

What message does the student get when we tell her that some of what we ask her to do is worth more than the rest of what we give her to do? Does weighting have any impact on student motivation? When we weight items/skills differently don't we automatically favor certain learning styles over others? What impact does the combination of averaging and weighting have on the validity of the grades our students are receiving?

With a standards-based, progress-based approach to scoring and reporting there is no weighting. Every power standard the student is working on is treated equally.

Composite Grading

Composite grading is when the teacher combines, usually by averaging, different skills and behaviors into one overall grade. For example, when a teacher combines test and quiz results, homework, attendance, and participation into one grade she is doing composite grading. A second example might be to combine test and quiz results, homework completion, neatness, and effort. Although each of these is related to the student's academic work they each involve a completely different set of skills.

Giving Zeros

I think it's safe to assume that we all agree that if there isn't a single thing "correct" on a piece of work a student turns in, then her score (as opposed to grade) for that particular piece of work is 0. That's just a quantitative reality.

And I think most of us agree that if students don't complete or hand in work that has been asked of them, then they should not be rewarded or awarded in any way for something they didn't follow through on.

I'm also guessing most of us agree with the concept of *natural consequences*. In the case of incomplete work, the natural consequence is to simply not give the student any credit for something he didn't do. Placing a value, which zero (0) is, on something that doesn't even exist is not a natural consequence. The simple fact is if a student doesn't complete or hand in work the work is incomplete ... period.

Zeros given as scores for completely incorrect work that is turned in are not the zeros that are problematic. It is zeros that are given for **incomplete** work that are the issue.

First, zeros have an unfair impact when averaged into final grades that are based on the traditional 100-90-80 etc. grading scheme. There are equal 10 point increments from 100-90-80-70-60-50 but a 49 point gap between 49 and 0.

Secondly, giving zeros is a form of punishment, but a score or grade is value and value is something that is rewarded or awarded, the opposite of punishment.

Related to this, threatening students with zeros is an extrinsic behaviorist tactic that is more about compliance and less about learning. There is no research supporting the notion that the threat of getting a zero or being punished with a zero increases a student's learning.

The Problem with Giving Zeros

Typically it is work assigned outside the classroom (i.e., homework) for which zeros come into play. There are many legitimate reasons, access and availability to name two, why students are unable to complete and/or turn in work assigned outside of school. For this reason giving zeros for incomplete homework is very often an ethical and equity issue.

Another issue with giving zeros is the message it sends. When we simply give students a zero and move on the message is that the work wasn't really all that important or critical to their learning. And if not, then why did we waste their and our time assigning it?

And by simply giving the students zeros and moving on we "let them off the hook." Again, the assignment must not have been all that important. And if the students can hold out and win the test of wills between them and their teacher the teacher will eventually give up, leave them alone, and in the end they get away with not having to do the work.

When we look at the arguments for giving zeros it's hard to dispute the fact that not one has anything to do with improving student learning. For the most part they simply boil down to punishment, compliance, and control.

We have several options for how to deal with students not completing or handing in work. We can continue to practice unnatural consequences and punish them with zeros. We can chase and hound them until they turn the work in, the quality of which is typically of the "just turn something in to avoid a zero" type. We can call the work incomplete and withhold from them something of real value (e.g., diploma, driver's education) until it is completed ... again, an unnatural consequence typically resulting in work of questionable worth. We can hold the student accountable not by letting incomplete work destroy their grade for the work they have done, but by having incomplete work be accounted for as part of their grade for a separate, related standard (e.g., a separate "effort," "responsibility," or "productivity" grade).

Or ... we can practice standards-based formative instruction and assessment and progress scoring. With this approach to teaching effort is built into the process and consequences for incomplete work are natural. If students choose to not take advantage of learning opportunities provided for them they will not be able to demonstrate sustained growth in the standards they're being assessed in, and that will naturally be reflected in the grade they receive. With this approach students own and are accountable for their learning.

And finally, there are deeper issues around the practice of giving zeros. First, the underlying assumption is that the threat of zeros is needed because without that threat students (human nature) will choose not to do their work because they are naturally lazy, tend toward ease and effortlessness, naturally rebel against compliance, tend to avoid unpleasantness and discomfort, etc. Second, because it is their nature to not do the work they need to be taught a lesson anytime that occurs, and the punishment a zero brings will do that. And third, related to both threat and punishment is one of our (teachers') "elephants in the room" ... control.

But learning is innate! We are literally (biochemically) wired to learn. We are innately curious, explorative and questioning, and we actually experience biochemical stimulation when we learn. And schools are places of learning. *So what is going on that innately curious learners, in places of learning, need to be threatened to take advantage of opportunities to learn?*

Is That an Evaluation or an Assessment?

Unfortunately, the term "assessment" is commonly misused and abused by practitioners and policymakers alike. The two terms are not synonymous and the two practices are antithetical to one another.

To determine whether something is a formative assessment or a summative evaluation all one has to do is see if there is a comparative cut-score grading scale being used. If the results obtained from the task completed by the student are categorized by being placed into some form of cut-score scale (A-B-C-D-F or 4-3-2-1 or 90th percentile-80th percentile, etc. or Beyond Standard-At Standard-Below Standard) and then that cut-score placement is acted on in some comparative or categorical way (i.e., reported, used for placement, used for tracking students, used to delineate competency, used to bestow honors or rewards, etc.) then the task is an **evaluation**.

Evaluations are used to categorize something's worth. Using a cut-score scale to categorize something's worth is a practice known as ***grading***. *Grading and evaluation are synonymous. Assessment and evaluation are not synonymous.* Assessment is simply the practice of gathering, on an ongoing basis, qualitative and quantitative information as a way to check for student progress/growth ... and then using that information to shape subsequent instruction in a way that further promotes student learning. There is no grading involved with formative assessment.

Tests such as NECAP, SAT, ACT, GED, TIMSS, and NAEP are not assessments. Although they are finally starting to be used as feedback for actually guiding teachers' subsequent instruction (some think of this as teaching toward next year's test, given when teachers typically get the results from these tests), they are still primarily used as evaluations.

Grades and High Stakes

Giving standardized tests is not the only high stakes practice we conduct in education. Evaluation, particularly the giving of grades, is just as high stakes, if not more. The short and long term impacts that grades have on individuals and the ripple effect those impacts have on society are far reaching. Some examples of the high stakes of grading are listed below.

- Grades positively, extrinsically motivate some students.
- They presumably reflect achievement and imply that learning has occurred.
- Grades presumably reflect achievement and imply degree of intelligence.
- They can be a source of stress and anxiety.
- Grades provide a premature appraisal of what a child has learned, will learn, and is capable of learning.
- They imply that there are acceptable/normal and unacceptable/below normal stages of progress and levels of learning, and that there are levels that are both better and best.
- Grades impact a child's self-esteem.
- They contribute to a child's identity.
- Grades categorize and stigmatize.
- They promote overt and covert tracking.
- Grades promote divisiveness in schools, families, and communities.

- They influence a child's future and future direction.
- Grades regulate a child's degree of opportunity.
- They contribute toward creating, reinforcing, and sustaining a class system (a "haves" and "have nots" society.
- Grading typically categorizes students based on their ability to meet someone else's expectations rather than their intrinsic ability to learn.
- It typically imposes a rigid, one-size-fits-all categorization process that does not accommodate all learning styles.
- Grading can promote an externally rather than internally-driven approach to learning.
- It serves as a negative rather than positive motivator for some students.
- Grading can inhibit/prohibit risk taking and alternative thinking.
- It can inhibit/prohibit the natural process of constructivist learning.

The first set of impacts occurs regardless of whether or not the grades being given are valid, reliable, and fair. The second set is common given the ways in which grading is typically done. Given the high stakes of grading and the unreliability, subjectivity, and flaws (e.g., averaging, unfair cut-score scales, weighting, composite grading, giving zeros) inherent in the way grading is typically done, is it a practice we want to continue to conduct in our classrooms?

~ III ~

CONSTRUCTIVIST LEARNING
AND PROGRESSIVE THINKING

Constructivist Learning

Throughout the remaining sections in this book are reflections on (and grounded in) constructivist learning theory. The "Trees Diagram" on the following page is referred or alluded to throughout these reflections. The diagram is an attempt to visually represent the following.

The children who come into our classroom come with diverse backgrounds all shaped by varying physiological, cultural, socio-economic, and psychological/emotional factors. Young children have no control over any of these background factors.

These factors, in complex interplay, all influence not only what children get to experience, but the degree to which they get to experience those things. In turn, those experiences are what shape their schemas/knowledge constructs (represented by the trees). Some students come into the classroom having relatively complex schemas, while others come in having relatively simple schemas.

Our students, whether well matched with the learning environment or not, all engage in the same general classroom experience and do so for the same duration of time. Yet despite knowing that the time it takes to construct knowledge depends on the complexity of our existing schemas and that that complexity, in turn, affects both our ability and availability to learn, we still continue to comparatively grade students based on their relative attainment within the same allotted time period (a unit, marking period, school year). Is it fair to sort and rank children and pit them against one another? From a social justice standpoint is it ethical?

Constructivist Learning Theory and Grading

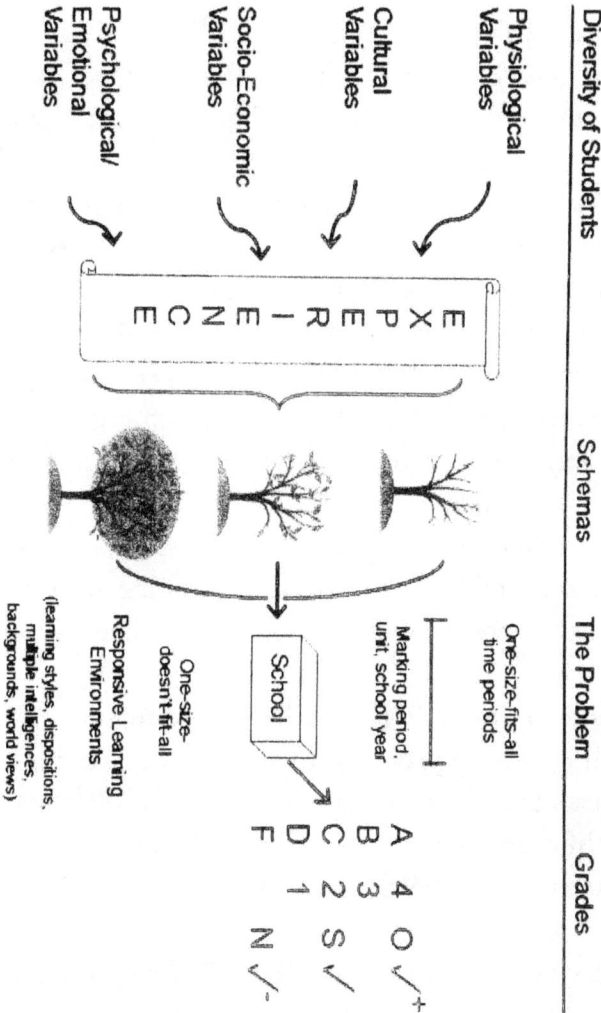

Diversity of Students	Schemas	The Problem	Grades

Physiological Variables

Cultural Variables

Socio-Economic Variables

Psychological/ Emotional Variables

EXPERIENCE

One-size-fits-all time periods

Marking period, unit, school year

One-size-doesn't-fit-all

School

Responsive Learning Environments

(learning styles, dispositions, multiple intelligences, backgrounds, world views)

A 4 O √+
B 3 S √
C 2
D 1 N √-
F

Constructivist Learning Theory (Continued)

Learning is an (inter)active, formative process shaped by social and experiential opportunities and interactions.

Knowledge, itself, is in a continual state of construction, deconstruction, and reconstruction.

The complexity of that construction depends on the frequency, amount, and diversity of connections (schematic connectivity) available for the learner to build upon.

The connections the learner makes will vary depending on the individual learner's physiological development, emotional availability, and cultural context.

As learners accommodate and assimilate experiences into their existing schemas they don't simply accumulate them as if throwing pennies into a jar. Each new experience melds in some way with their existing schema, forever changing both the schema and the new experience into an entity completely different than their original respective forms. And what new construct emerges varies from one learner to the next because of their diverse schemas and what each new experience has to connect with.

Some of those factors that shape the learner's opportunity, readiness, and availability to construct knowledge are identifiable and some are not; some are within the learner's control but many are not.

Learning is a uniquely individualized phenomenon, a process through which everyone proceeds in unique ways and at varying rates. This raises the question, is evaluating (grading and norm-referencing) children within one-size-fits-all time spans (e.g., the length of a marking period) valid and fair?

Constructivist Learning: Some "Final" Thoughts (For Now, Anyway)

Each one of us learns in different ways, at different rates, and at different times in our lives. The rate at which we construct our personal body of knowledge and the extent to which we build upon that knowledge (i.e., our individual growth/progress) varies due to a multitude of interacting factors, many of which we have no control over.

Our students' cultural, social, emotional, physiological, and socio-economic makeups are as different from one another as their fingerprints. Consequently, our students' prior opportunities for learning and present access to learning vary widely, which in turn means their readiness to learn and availability for learning are also as different from one another as their fingerprints.

Learning is a process. It is something that progresses over time and never stops. There is no finality to learning. And, learning is a process that is influenced by our breadth and depth of experience, the diversity of our social interactions, our physiological and psychological makeup, and the cultural filters through which we experience our experiences. Learning is contextual.

Experiential, social, physiological/psychological, and cultural factors influence our rate of schema development, which in turn influences the rate at which we learn, and so on. The time it takes to learn and the optimal context in which to learn naturally and widely vary from one individual to the next.

A Teacher to His Students

I come here with a complicated construct that governs my personality, bias, vocabulary, style, and methodology, the combination of which may "work" well (motivate, intrigue, promote a sense of trust, encourage risk taking) for some of you (and your unique and complicated constructs) but not so well for others. That's just human nature, but an aspect of the student-teacher relationship that critically affects students both short and long term.

As we witnessed during last night's group work each of us comes to this course with completely different levels of knowledge, understanding, and experience with standards-based formative instruction and assessment ... and grading. And our varying life experiences are going to regulate our individual readiness for what we'll be exploring in this course, and our varying backgrounds are going to influence our openness to dissonance, and consequently our availability for new learning. That's not a judgment. It's just a matter-of-fact statement of the reality of learning and the learner.

Not only do our varying life experiences and backgrounds place each of us on different learning curves, but so do our present situations. What we teach, how many students we teach, how much contact time we have with our students, how much flexibility we have with our curriculum, etc., etc., etc. will impact the rate at which each of us is going to be able to assimilate, accommodate, apply, and ultimately transform the subject matter we'll be exploring in this course. And of course the demands our unique personal lives have on our professional lives will affect our progress as well.

We are not all starting out on a level playing field with regard to our readiness and availability to learn, yet we will all be getting "taught" the same content by the same teacher, engage in relatively similar learning opportunities, and will be given the exact same amount of time (two months) to grow our knowledge and understanding of what's being taught.

Given all of this, how could it possibly be valid, reliable, fair, and not discriminatory if I were to 1) determine what I believe qualifies as A work vs. B or less work, 2) personally judge the value of your work, and 3) then grade you accordingly?

Radical Reform?

The reform (progress-based scoring and reporting) that we are exploring is, without a doubt, radical. It is radical not in the revolutionary sense of the word but in its literal sense. The root meaning of radical is *root* and the change we are talking about is, indeed, getting back to the root. How? Because the root word of education is *educe*, which means to draw out. "Draw out" implies that every child has potential and can and does learn. But we know that no two children's schemas, learning styles, and learning curves are alike or equal, and never will be. Doesn't "drawing out" of every child imply the need for individualized progress-based scoring rather than comparative attainment-based grading?

Philosophical Orientation?

Where you are in the following philosophical continua will influence how you interact with the standards-based, progress-based scoring, grading, and reporting reforms being discussed in this book.

Do you believe in:

Competition *or* Cooperation/Collaboration

Independence *or* Interdependence

Behaviorism *or* Constructivism

Attainment *or* Progress

Norm-referencing *or* Criterion-referencing

Absolutism *or* Relativism

Preserving status quo *or* Promoting change

Conservative *or* Progressive

Winners and losers *or* Players

Shifts in Thinking, Shifts in Practice

Research in cognitive science, constructivist learning, and formative assessment is pushing us to think differently about teaching and learning. Some of those shifts are listed below.

Making the shift from ...

- focusing on teaching to focusing on student learning
- covering factual content to helping students internalize generalized concepts and skills
- stressing information retention to stressing knowledge construction
- conducting mostly summative evaluation to conducting mostly formative assessment
- believing there is finality in acquiring knowledge to believing there is no finality in learning

- norm-referenced grading and reporting to criterion-referenced scoring and reporting
- assigning grades to reporting scores
- honoring attainment to honoring progress (achievement)
- grading based on meeting/not meeting a standard to grading based on sustained progress toward meeting a standard
- instruction and assessment to instruction is assessment and vice versa
- grading the student's work to grading the student's progress
- thinking that all students can learn equally to thinking that all students can learn, but don't learn equally

The Term "Formative"

The term "formative" describes never-ending processes:

- of shaping ("*forming*") and being shaped ("*formed*") by
- that are ongoing, continuous, and for which there is no finality
- that are cyclical, not linear
- that involve feedback loops (i.e., are in*formative*)
- of consequent and subsequent responsiveness
- of continuous adaptation and evolution (trans*formative*)

"Formative Assessment"

The term formative assessment is actually redundant. Internal to any system are natural feedback loops that continually regulate the inner working of the system. Feedback is information and "loops" illustrates the cyclical nature of that feedback. In other words, systems naturally engage in internal self-assessment, with that information continually shaping and in turn being shaped by the inner workings of the system, hence the term formative. Assessment *is* formative.

This redundancy is actually a blessing because it helps expose abuse of the term assessment. Assessment and evaluation are not synonymous yet they are routinely recklessly used that way. The two terms are antithetical. Assessment is the formative process described above. An example is a teacher drawing out a student's competency in order to learn how to further that student's competency. Evaluation is summative. It's grading ... using a cut-score grading scale to comparatively judge, rank, and place value on a student based on their attainment (or not) of norms. Standardized tests are not assessments, so-called standards-based report cards that rate students as "At Standard" or not are evaluations, and the term "summative assessment" is an oxymoron.

There can be no such thing as a "summative" assessment or a summative "assessment." If it is summative then it's not formative. And, according to both the etymology and systems theory definitions of the terms formative and assessment, if it's not formative then it's not an assessment.

And finally, it is impossible to talk about formative assessment without also talking about formative instruction. One cannot happen in isolation from the other. As is the case with "teaching and learning," formative instruction and assessment is a single entity. Assessment is embedded in instruction. Instruction instructs and assesses simultaneously.

"Formative Assessment" (Continued)

Regularly checking for understanding with our students is one aspect of formative assessment. Periodically monitoring their progress over time using a multi-faceted mix of assessments and when meaningful the same assessment activity is also part of formative assessment. And, rather than grading each of those assignments simply using them as means for providing both student and teacher with feedback is a third aspect of formative assessment. A fourth is periodically measuring a student's current body of work up against a progress rubric (see Section Five).

But there's more to formative assessment than that. Our understanding of the term "formative assessment" exposes a shortcoming in the way we commonly think and speak about the practice. It is technically impossible for there to be just "formative assessment." The assessment isn't formative unless it has a coevolving partner. That partner, in this case, is instruction. Assessment isn't formative unless it's part of formative instruction and assessment.

It is formative instruction and assessment that constructivist learning and education research is promoting. Simply doing those four things listed above is only half the process. Continual assessment must be continually shaping subsequent instruction, with subsequent instruction in turn continually shaping subsequent assessment, and so on. If our "formative assessment" isn't genuinely dictating what and how we teach so as to further our students' understanding and skill level beyond that revealed by our latest assessment, then we aren't really doing true formative assessment.

Progress vs. Attainment ... and Achievement

Both progress and attainment constitute achievement. When a student shows growth and has made *progress* in her acquisition of knowledge and skills, that growth is an achievement worth recognizing and honoring. When a student has *attained* a particular level of competency he has achieved something as well.

Progress equates to growth. Progress is inherent to standards-based instruction as well as standards-based formative assessment. As a student continually strives toward "meeting" a standard (a rigorous expectation, an ideal) and along the way is attaining escalating levels of competency in that standard, the student is going through a process. And anytime a process is occurring progress is inherently occurring as well. Progress is an organic element of standards-based instruction.

Progress is also an organic element of formative assessment. The term formative essentially means to shape and be shaped by. In the context of education, formative instruction and assessment refers to the cyclical (not linear) process of teaching and learning. The standards shape our instruction. The results of the formative assessment embedded in that instruction shape our subsequent instruction, which in turn shapes our next round of formative assessment, and so on. This responsive cycle of shaping and being shaped by is an ongoing process and again, process inherently involves progress.

Attainment, on the other hand, implies finality. When a student has attained a particular level of competency they have "*finally*" gotten to that level and as they move on toward the next level of attainment the previous level of attainment, which was a temporal *finish* line, is now left behind as a temporal starting line. That level of attainment was a short term destination. **In essence, that level of attainment was simply just one more level of progress.** This raises two questions. Is there truly any such thing as attainment? Is true attainment actually attainable?

Constructivist learning reveals that learning is the process of knowledge construction, and that with every experiential connection the learner makes that experience is, in some way, assimilated and accommodated into the learner's existing but ever-expanding construct of knowledge. In other words, there is no finality in learning. The learner's schema is in an infinite state of construction, deconstruction, and reconstruction. So again, is there truly such a thing as attainment or is it simply progress? And if it is simply progress, is "attainment" worthy of high stakes evaluation?

"Attainment?"

Let's consider this concept of attainment at the simplest level ... recall. Our students either know it or they don't, right? We employ a variety of tactics to get kids to memorize something. Eventually, or not, we get to the point where we say, "Yes! They got (attained) it! Yippee!" Then after a while of not having to recall or use it, they no longer can recall it. So if they can't recall it, did they ever really attain it?

Additional Thoughts on "Attainment"

Is "attainment" simply an illusion? Ecology, constructivism, and phenomenology reveal that everything is in a constant state of evolution and everything is infinitely nested. In other words, nothing is static or finite. There is always another level, layer, or degree. Hence, there is no finality in learning and thus true attainment is unobtainable. Therefore, any time we set a standard that we hope our students will attain all we are doing is simply setting and defining a level of proficiency that we believe is "good enough." We are simply marking a "finish" line at an arbitrary point along an eternal course of *progress*.

Can Anything Ever Truly be Summative?

The concept of formative comes from systems theory. It describes the never ending *transformative* process in which an entity is shaping the things around it while at the same time being shaped by those very things it's shaping.

In our assessment course we looked at how the standards, instruction and assessment, and teaching and learning are formative. There isn't a summative "bone in any of their bodies" ... which warrants the argument that summative evaluation (grading) has no place in education.

Some argue that in actuality everything is formative because everything is interdependent. Everything, directly or indirectly, largely or minutely, affects everything else, and in turn is affected by everything else. And even once an entity ceases to exist in its present form, its impact from having existed and the impact of its disappearance both have a lasting ripple effect on everything else ... a *transformative* ripple effect.

Transformation means markedly evolved in form or appearance, and evolved means having advanced toward greater sustainability. So with "formative," "transformative," and "evolution" in mind let's consider grades and grading.

Grades are summative. They are not formative because a) they are static, b) they are instantly obsolete upon providing the student with feedback (see Section Four), and c) although they may have a shaping impact on a student the student, in turn, is not able to shape them. The student can shape his overall average, but he can't shape those individual grades.

Essential Understandings

The following understandings are vitally important relative to standards-based, progress-based scoring, grading, and reporting (see Sections Four and Five).

Constructivist Learning

Recognizing and accepting that true learning is all about the construction of knowledge, not simply the retention of information, and that there is no finality in true learning. True learning is ever-evolving and in a continual state of construction, which can only happen as long as continual opportunities to make more and more connections are being provided to the learner.

Constructivism vs. Behaviorism

Recognizing and accepting that the goal is to continually draw out the students' understanding, not simply to bombard them with information and tactics to try and manipulate their retention of that information. The primary focus should be on their learning, not our teaching.

Backwards Design

Planning instruction by starting with the standards, their criteria, and their respective progress rubrics for those standards that clearly define the standards' criteria and performance benchmarks, rather than starting out with a focus on existing scope and sequence content, units, and lessons.

Criteria-based Learning Activities

Purposefully developing enabling activities based on the actual criteria listed on the generalized-standard progress rubrics; activities that will automatically draw out student demonstration of those very criteria for which the teacher is trying to assess student progress.

Multiple Opportunities

Recognizing and accepting that knowledge construction (as opposed to simple information retention) requires that students be provided multiple opportunities over time and across contexts to work on a given standard ... mile deep immersion rather than mile wide coverage.

Formative Assessment

Continually gathering the evidence (student work) that results from those multiple criteria-based enabling activities and periodically using the most current accumulation of that evidence to measure (up against the rubric) the student's evolving proficiency in those criteria (standards) ... that versus evaluating (grading) everything the student does and then averaging those grades into one overall grade.

Scoring vs. Grading

Recognizing and accepting that scoring is simply that ... scoring ... and grading, as revealed by constructivist learning theory is arguably a discriminatory practice.

Content-based vs. Standards-based Instruction

Content-based instruction is linear. It typically involves teaching particular topics or units in a "one right after the other" sequence. When one unit is completed the teacher then moves on to the next. Sometimes connections are made between units but typically the units are treated as separate entities. The unit that was just completed is left behind as the teacher moves on to the next unit.

Standards-based instruction is cyclical. A standard is continuously taught, reinforced, practiced, and re-engaged in as the teacher moves from one topic or unit to the next. Students are given multiple opportunities to work on a standard within the context of a particular unit, and then when that unit is completed and the teacher moves on to the next topic the same standard is again addressed, reinforced, and practiced within that new context. The standard is never left behind and an escalating spiral of growth in competency occurs as the student continually engages and re-engages in the standard.

System theory reveals that all systems are inherently cyclical and that linear processes are unable to sustain themselves. It is the cyclical processes within a system that sustain the system itself. Constructivist learning theory, a systems theory relative to learning and knowledge construction, confirms that learning (knowledge construction, schema development) is a cyclical process. From a systems and constructivist standpoint, standards-based instruction and assessment is a more natural and appropriate approach to teaching and learning than is content-based instruction.

Proposition
Grade "A" meat is only Grade "A" for a nanosecond at most.

~ IV ~

A LOGICAL SYNTHESIS

The ABC's of Social Injustice: An Indictment of Grading

Dear Danny ... and Candace ... and Chamonix ... and .... I am so sorry I did not know as a young teacher what I now know about grading.

For twelve years I taught at the middle school level, and without thinking much about it my first two years I simply did what most teachers do. I graded my students the way I was graded in school.

By the end of my second year, however, I noticed that I had begun dreading the onset of report card season. And when reporting time came I would spend days agonizing over coming up with grades for my students that I felt were valid and justified. Recognizing this angst launched me into what was to become my life's work in education. I started seriously reflecting not just on my own grading methods, but on the concept of grading itself. By year five of my career I was on my fourth approach to grading.

That, in itself, raises questions about the validity of grades and the reliability of grading practices. If we continually tinker with our grading policies, which most teachers do because instinctively we know something's not quite right about grading, then what does that mean about the validity of the grades we gave prior to our tinkering? But there's much more.

After twelve years as a middle school teacher I took a different path. But my questions about grading continued. My new position was teaching ecology courses for teachers.

Through ecology I rediscovered constructivist learning. I recognized the interdependence between teaching and learning and that teaching-and-learning is actually a *formative* process; a continuous process where teaching shapes student learning and, in turn, student learning shapes subsequent teaching. Or at least it should if we want the process to be a sustainable one.

At that same time brain-based research was flooding us with new information on how the brain works and what impacts how and when learning occurs. Cognitive science was confirming what constructivists had been saying for decades ... that learning is a formative, constructive process. The mismatch between learning and grading was becoming more and more glaring to me.

If teaching-and-learning is formative, and the construction of knowledge is a never ending process, then what role does anything summative, like grading, have in education? Isn't grading the antithesis of all we know about teaching and learning? My instinct about grading had by then moved to skepticism and my sense of alarm was becoming a conviction. That passion eventually landed me in my next position. For sixteen years I taught courses designed to allow educators to uncover the fallacy of grading. What follows is an attempt to capture that work in a nutshell.

Grading is the highest stakes thing we do in education. Grades label and stigmatize children. They are divisive. They become a child's identity. They impact a child's self-worth and self-esteem. *And they regulate a child's opportunities both during and beyond their school years.* That's troubling enough. Pile on top of that the issues we're about to look at and ... well, quite frankly I'm amazed we educators are not defendants in the world's largest class action lawsuit ever filed.

Grading students is a social justice issue. It's an ethical issue, if not a moral one. It's a practice we can no longer deny needs to stop.

For starters, grading students is an inherently discriminatory process. There are many factors that regulate and shape a child's schema. The culture they are raised in and their family's socio-economic status affect not just what they get to experience growing up, but the degree to which they get to experience it. Experience is what fuels the cognitive connections we're able to make, and making connections is what grows our schemas. The children coming into our classrooms are naturally at different stages of readiness to learn. They also come with varying physiological, psychological, and emotional attributes impacting both their access to learning as well as their availability to learn.

Children have no control over these factors. They do not choose to be born into their family's culture or to be raised in the socioeconomic conditions they grow up in. And they do not choose their physiological, psychological, and emotional make ups.

So how is grading discriminatory? We know that students enter our classrooms with schemas that are as different from one another as their fingerprints. And that means they all come in at different levels of readiness to learn. They also come in having had different degrees of access to learning and with different levels of availability for learning. They can't possibly experience a lesson in the same way or learn the material at the same rate.

But "school" is organized in fixed time frames ... the length of a unit, a marking period, a school year. And at the end of each of those set time periods students receive a grade. Those set time periods are in effect one-size-fits-all time allotments for learning. So even though we know our incoming students are not all on the same "starting line," we comparatively rank them against the same "finish line." But children do not choose their "starting lines." That is why grading is discriminatory.

A second but related reason why grading is a social justice issue is teachers. Everything I just described applies to us as well. We, too, enter our classrooms with schemas shaped by our unique backgrounds. That means we come with a set bias and a subjective perspective. For that reason we can never be equally responsive to the array of students sitting in our classrooms. It's impossible. Some students will thrive with us and others won't. And then comes time for us to give them all grades. To grade means to evaluate, and the root word of evaluate means to judge. So we are now the judge, but a biased and subjective one. And that is an equity issue.

The fact that learning is a formative process but grading is summative is a persuasive *theoretical* argument for ending grading. And the fact that grading is discriminatory, teachers are naturally biased, and grading is subjective are compelling *ethical* arguments for abandoning grading.

There is a third equally urgent reason to do away with grading. The ways in which we concoct grades – averaging, weighting, composite grading, giving zeros, and use of random cut-score grading scales – are all seriously flawed and ultimately discriminatory as well. But before we look at that there's a second grading "ah-ha" (the first being grading is discriminatory) that teachers who look closely at grading invariably experience.

If we correct a student's work, score it (for example, +43/50), grade it (for example, +43/50 = B+), write instructive comments on it to help the student further learn the topic of that work, and then return it to the student as feedback, the instant the student interacts with that feedback her knowledge of that topic changes ... *and consequently the grade is instantly obsolete.* So if we truly are using student work formatively, which research confirms is effective teaching, then what are we doing with all those obsolete grades, and what purpose is it serving to even give those grades in the first place?

This "ah-ha" segues nicely into looking at what is perhaps the most seriously flawed of the five grading practices mentioned above ... averaging students' grades.

When we average we take our most current measure of student learning and combine it with a number of older measures. We take the student's most current grade and dilute it with previous grades the student received when his knowledge was the product of less and even lesser experiences. But with each new experience the student had after receiving those earlier grades his schema advanced. Consequently, an average does not reflect a student's actual proficiency at the time.

Furthermore, averaging is regressive. The impact each successive grade has on a student's average incrementally lessens over time. Basically what that means is students who come in "more advanced" have an advantage over others, even those whose learning accelerates later in the year and whose knowledge may end up surpassing that of those "more advanced" students.

As stated earlier, there are legitimate reasons why students don't all come into a classroom at the same "starting line" and why students don't all learn at the same time, in the same way, and at the same rate. As with grading in general, averaging is both a theoretical and ethical issue. It is out of synch with what brain research has revealed about learning and it is discriminatory because it favors students who are more ready and available to learn than others.

Weighting, composite grading, giving zeros, and use of random cut-score-grading scales are flawed grading practices as well. When we weight items differently we favor certain learning styles. For example, if tests are worth 65% of the final grade, those whose learning style aligns with test taking will have an advantage. If weighting isn't discriminatory, it's at least prejudicial.

Composite grading, which typically involves weighting, is the practice of taking things like test scores, homework completion, participation, neatness, etc. and combining those scores into one grade. But composite grades don't tell us what a child actually knows or is able to do, or to what degree.

Giving zeros for incomplete work is problematic, too. First, it is generally assignments outside the classroom that end up as incomplete work, and there are many legitimate reasons why some students are more at a disadvantage when it comes to completing homework than others. Again, discrimination is an issue here.

Giving zeros is also unfair because there are ten point increments from 100% - 90% - 80% - 70% - 60% but a 59 point increment from 59 to 0. Just one zero unfairly skews a child's overall grade, which is especially unfair because that zero isn't even a reflection of the student's knowledge. It may be a reflection of some other skill such as responsibility, organization, or motivation. Far too often it is simply a reflection of some type of after-school hardship.

And finally, use of random cut-score grading scales raises validity and reliability questions as well. If we sometimes use the traditional 100% - 90% - 80% scale, other times the natural gap scale (student scores are put in order and where there's a significant gap between one block of scores and the next, that's where the cut is made), and still other times an adjusted scale (the highest scores get the A's and we work down from there), then how can we say *any* of those grades are valid?

Grading is discriminatory, subjective, fallacious, and flawed. Do we really need any more reasons to do away with grading? And when we do finally abandon grading, we won't be lacking when it comes to measuring and reporting student learning. There are valid, reliable, and non-discriminatory ways to do that. For example, not a single problem addressed in this article applies when we simply monitor and report student growth on an individual basis using the students' ongoing *progress scores*. For instance, if a student is showing growth in 7 of the 12 skills she's working on, her progress score is 7 out of 12 or 7/12 or 58% ... period. Progress scoring aligns with how learning works and does not discriminate against students.

In his 1970 book, *Deschooling Society*, Ivan Illich reveals the fallacy of "school." The general public is not yet ready to go as far as Illich advocates but a growing number are rethinking school and justifiably so. Why? Well, let's take grading for example ...

Logical Deduction

Three areas of study that have contributed greatly to our understanding of learning and how to validly and reliably assess one's learning are cognitive science, motivation theory, and objective measurement. A synthesis of this research reveals a significant disconnect between how learning occurs, formative assessment of learning, and grading. A logical deduction from this synthesis is that grading is an act of social injustice.

For those interested in pursuing this issue further, the following bibliography of historical groundwork will provide a start.

Cognitive Science

Caine, R.N. & Caine, G. (1994). *Making Connections: Teaching and the Human Brain*. Alexandria, VA: ASCD.

Wolfe, P. (2001). *Brain Matters: Translating Research into Classroom Practice*. Alexandria, VA: ASCD.

Motivation Theory

Butler, R. (1988). Enhancing and undermining intrinsic motivation: The effects of task-involving and ego-involving evaluation on interest and performance. *British Journal of Educational Psychology*, 58, 1-14.

Crooks, T.J. (1988). The impact of classroom evaluation practices on students. *Review of Educational Research*, 58, 438-481.

Deutsch, M. (1979). Education and distributive justice: Some reflections on grading systems. *American Psychologist*, 34 (5), 391-401.

Dweck, C. (1992). Achievement goals and intrinsic motivation: Their relation and their role in adaptive motivation. *Motivation and Emotion*, 16 (3), 231-247.

Natriello, G. (1987). The impact of evaluation processes on students. *Educational Psychologist*, 22 (2), 155-175.

Tomlinson, C.A. (2001). Grading for success. *Educational Leadership*, 3, 12-15.

Measurement

Black, P. & Wiliam, D. (1998). Inside the black box: Raising standards through classroom assessment. *Phi Delta Kappan*, 10, 139-148.

Brookhart, S.M. (2009). *Grading.* New York, NY: Pearson.

__(2008). *How to Give Effective Feedback to Your Students.* Alexandria, VA: ASCD.

__(2004). Classroom Assessment: Tensions and intersections in theory and practice. *Teachers College Record,* 106(3), 429-458.

__(1994). Teachers' grading: Practice and Theory. *Applied Measurement in Education,* 7 (4), 279-301.

__(1993). Teachers' grading practices: Meaning and values. *Journal of Educational Measurement,* 30 (2), 123-142.

Delandshere, G. (2002). Assessment as inquiry. *Teachers College Record,* 104 (7), 1461-1484.

Glaser, R. (1981). The future of testing: A research agenda for cognitive psychology and psychometrics. *American Psychologist,* 36, 924.

Johnston, P. (1989). Constructive evaluation and the improvement of teaching and learning. *Teachers College Record,* 90 (4), 509-528.

Grading Aha #1 Relative to Constructivist Learning

When students' scores (e.g., 15/20 or 75%) are inserted into a comparative cut-score grading scale (A-B-C-D-F; 4-3-2-1; Beyond Standard-At Standard-Below Standard) and converted to grades at the conclusion of a set time frame such as a marking period, students end up being ranked against a common timed finish line *despite not all being on the same starting line (schematically) at the beginning of the marking period.* Based on what cognitive science and constructivism reveal about how learning occurs and all the contextual variables that shape and regulate one's knowledge construction and schema development, how can grading not be a discriminatory process?

From Grading to Discrimination

Whenever we grade that automatically means we are using a cut-score grading scale of some kind. Anytime we use a cut-score grading scale that means we are grading the student based on what they have attained or their level of attainment. For example, if we give a student a B what we are saying is that the student has attained a B's worth of competency. And anytime we grade students based on their attainment (as opposed to their progress) that means we are norm-referencing (comparing them to some norm).

If we agree with what cognitive science and constructivism reveal about learning and knowledge construction, when we grade students based on attainment of a particular norm we are automatically discriminating against a percentage of our students. Grading based on comparative attainment of a norm is an inherently discriminatory practice.

How is Grading Discriminatory? Let's Look at the Whole

Students are mandated to attend particular schools and be taught by particular teachers. Teachers tend to reflect the schools/ classrooms in which they were schooled, and in turn tend to reinforce and perpetuate the same style of "schooling" where they teach.

Students are subjected to instruction, assessment, and evaluation practices that are direct manifestations of the cultural biases and physiological developmental curves of their individual teachers ... practices stemming from mental models that might not align with or accommodate the mental models of those students. The physiological developmental curves and cultural biases of some students will match those of their teachers better than others' will.

All students learn in different ways and at different rates, construct understandings unique to their existing schemas, and best express what they know in different ways as well.

Norms are one-size-fits-all expectations determined through the cultural and developmental lenses of a particular authority. Students of a similar developmental and cultural makeup will have less trouble meeting those norms than those with different developmental and cultural makeups.

The concept of norms is ethnocentric, imperialistic, oriented toward standardization, and conformist in nature. They go against what systems theory reveals is natural, that being a continual evolution toward diversity.

The origin and subsequent purpose of grading is to quantitatively compare, sort, and categorize. Grading based on attainment of developmental and cultural norms will result in a bell curve on which those whose culture and learning styles match those from which the norms originated will score high and those whose don't will score low.

Grades are presumed to be valid and reliable quantitative summations of a student's competence. Those with high grades are afforded greater opportunity (e.g., going on to become teachers) than those with low grades. The advantaged become more advantaged and the gap between classes persists.

If we are unwilling to "deschool" society, for the sake of all children let's at least "de-grade" school. If we are unwilling to "de-grade" school, for the sake of all children let's at least extinguish use of the term and concept of norms, or at least replace it with something less prescriptive and pejorative (e.g., ideals). Let's stop grading students based on attainment and start grading them based on individual progress (see Section Five).

Norms equal selection and selection equals discrimination because of the number of *uncontrollable* variables that uniquely influence every individual's ability to learn and availability for learning. The bottom line is attainment automatically means norms Are norms in any way consistent with constructivist learning?

Dissonance over Grading:
Constructivist Theory Reveals Why

Grades and grading practices are a constant source of tension for students, parents, and teachers. When one looks at grading through the lenses of constructivism and social justice, it quickly becomes evident why. This article explores the discrimination inherent in grading and the mismatch between grading and what constructivist learning theory reveals about the learner and knowledge construction, particularly around the systems notion of formative. An alternative to traditional grading is described.

"I absolutely dread report card time."

"Instinctively I know something's not right with the way I grade."

"I want to change the way we grade but I feel pressure not to."

Countless teachers I talk to express these and other concerns over grading. And the more approaches they try, and new approaches they read about, the more discouraged they get, which partly explains why traditional grading remains the status quo. *Perhaps the reason for this angst has nothing to do with right or wrong approaches to grading, but grading itself.* Before we examine this proposition, let's first step back and look at the broader context.

Contemporaries in education (see bibliography) are imploring us to think differently about teaching and learning. A number of those shifts in thinking and, in turn, practice are listed in Table 1, and each is connected in some way to grading.

Table 1: Shifts in Thinking, Shifts in Practice

FROM	TO
Focusing on our teaching	Focusing on our students' learning
Relying primarily on behaviorist notions about learning	Relying primarily on constructivist notions about learning
Simply covering factual content	Helping students toward proficiency in the standards
Stressing information retention	Stressing knowledge construction

Believing assessment and evaluation are synonymous	Recognizing assessment and evaluation are antithetical
Conducting mostly summative evaluation	Conducting mostly formative assessment
Believing there is finality in acquiring knowledge	Believing there is no finality in learning
Practicing norm-referenced grading and reporting	Practicing criterion-referenced grading and reporting
Assigning grades	Reporting scores
Honoring attainment	Honoring progress
Grading based on meeting/not meeting a standard	Grading based on sustained progress in the standards
Planning for instruction and then assessment	Recognizing instruction is assessment and vice versa
Grading the students' work	Grading the students' progress
Thinking all students can learn uniformly	Believing all students can learn but don't learn uniformly

Three shifts in practice that are having a major impact on classrooms today are standards-based instruction, formative assessment, and differentiated instruction and it is hard to find a reflective educator who is not evolving toward all three. And yet, despite progressive advances such as these, grading, the most high stakes practice in education, and the practice with which all of these practices culminate remains static ... a disconnect that is both striking and distressing (Dunn, et. al., 2007).

How to validly and effectively grade students, and whether we should even be grading them, has been an issue of contention in education for decades (Guskey, 1994; Kohn, 1996). Our current emphasis on standards-based instruction and formative assessment is pushing us to look at this issue perhaps harder than ever before. The purpose of this article is to weigh in with one more voice on grading. However, before addressing grading it will be helpful to first look at some of the concepts listed in Table 1 that are fundamental to the issue. Although everything listed in Table 1 relates to grading, we will look specifically at formative assessment vs. summative evaluation, progress vs. attainment, standards-based instruction, constructivist learning, and scoring vs. grading.

Formative Assessment vs. Summative Evaluation

The term assessment comes from the root word *assidere*, which means to sit beside and assist (Herman, et. al., 1992). Assessment is the process of working alongside students, monitoring their progress and providing ongoing feedback as they construct meaning and perpetuate their innate curiosity.

Formative assessment is the process of continually monitoring and measuring learning as it emerges and develops (*"forms"*), while at the same time continually gathering feedback and responding to that feedback in a way that shapes (*"forms"*) both the learner's subsequent learning and the teacher's subsequent instruction. It is a never ending cycle in which teaching and learning both shape and are shaped by one another.

Said differently, formative assessment is the ongoing gathering and documentation of information for the sole purpose of following student growth in learning. It is purposeful, provides meaningful feedback, influences lesson planning, directs subsequent instruction, prepares students to perform well when it comes time for evaluation, and assists students in progressing toward greater proficiency in the standards. Formative assessment is a qualitative process of guiding students as their learning *evolves* (emphasis intentional).

The term evaluation comes from the root words *valu*, which means to judge, determine a worth for, place a value on, appraise, grade, and *valere*, which means strength (Dunn, et. al., 2007). Evaluation is a process used to attempt to capture and define something's worth by comparatively categorizing it and then assigning it a *fixed* (emphasis intentional) value.

Summative evaluation is the practice of periodically attempting to sum, rank, and then assign value to the learner's overall ability at a given point in time. In other words, evaluation is the process of **grading** a student's competency or the worth of her work. It is a final (emphasis intentional) judgment of a student's performance or ability. Unlike assessment (monitoring growth), evaluation (grading) is strictly a summative process. Evaluation, summative evaluation, and grading are all synonymous.

As we can see, assessment and evaluation (grading) are in no way synonymous, and are not terms that can or should be used interchangeably. In fact, the two practices are antithetical.

Progress vs. Attainment

Both progress and attainment constitute achievement. When a student shows growth and has made progress in her acquisition of knowledge and skills, that growth is an achievement worth rewarding. Attaining a particular level of competency is an achievement, as well.

Progress equates to growth and is inherent in standards-based instruction as well as formative assessment. Standards are lifelong learning skills and concepts that entail knowledge construction, not simply information retention. And with construction of knowledge there is no finality, and therefore there is no finality with any of the standards. As a student continually evolves toward "meeting" a standard, and along the way is achieving escalating levels of competency in that standard, the student is going through a process. And anytime a process is occurring, progress is naturally occurring as well. *Progress is inherent in standards-based instruction.*

Progress is also inherent in formative assessment. The term "formative" essentially means to shape and be shaped by. In the context of education, formative instruction and assessment refers to the cyclical process of teaching and learning. The standards shape our instruction, the results of the formative assessment that's embedded in that instruction shape our subsequent instruction, which in turn shapes our next round of formative assessment, and so on. This responsive cycle of shaping and being shaped by is a process, and therefore naturally involves progress.

As with standards-based instruction and formative assessment progress is also intrinsic to constructivist learning. Constructivist learning theory reveals that learning is an act of constructing knowledge (Caine & Caine, 1994). With every interaction the learner has, that experience is in some way assimilated and accommodated into the learner's existing but ever-expanding construct of knowledge (more on constructivist learning shortly). In other words, there is no finality in learning. The learner's construct of knowledge is in an infinite state of construction, deconstruction, and reconstruction. Constructing knowledge is a process, which again, automatically entails progress.

Attainment, on the other hand, implies finality. When a student has attained a particular level of competency she has "finally" gotten to that level. As she moves on toward the next level of attainment the previous level of attainment, which in hindsight was only a temporal "finish" line, is now left behind as a temporal starting line. That level of attainment was only a short-term destination. In other words, that level of attainment was simply just one more degree of progress. And so, is there truly any such thing as attainment? Is true attainment actually attainable? And if "attainment" is simply progress, what value is there in grading students based on their attainment?

Because there is no finality in learning or with any standard, attainment can only ever be relative, and complete "attainment" is impossible. "Attaining the standard," "achieving the standard," "meeting the standard," and being "at standard" are all notions based simply on some level of proficiency someone has deemed sufficient. The proficiency labels are arbitrary, premature finish lines inserted into one's continuous learning curve. *Given how inherent progress is to teaching and learning it is fair to question why student progress, rather than student attainment, isn't our primary focus when it comes to instruction, assessment, evaluation, and reporting of student learning.*

Constructivist Learning

Constructivist learning theorists include Piaget, Bruner, and Vygotsky to name just a few (Brooks & Brooks, 1993). The following are some key notions that constructivists propose about learners and how learning occurs.

- Learning is an (inter)active, formative process shaped by social and experiential interactions.
- Knowledge, itself, is in a continual state of (de)(re)construction.
- The complexity of one's construct depends on the amount of connections available for the learner to build upon.
- The degrees of connectivity that exist within different learners' schemas depend on their experiential bases.
- The connections that individual learners make while constructing knowledge vary depending on the influence of their physiological development, emotional availability, and social and culture contexts.
- As learners accommodate/assimilate experiences into their existing schemas, they don't simply accumulate them as if throwing pennies into a jar. Each new experience that's assimilated melds in some unique way with their existing knowledge constructs, forever changing both the construct and the new experience into entities completely different from their original form. Those new constructs that emerge

naturally vary from one learner to the next because of their different founding experiences. Those differences grow exponentially as new experiences continue to be assimilated differently into already differing schemas.

- Some of the specific factors that regulate a learner's readiness and availability to learn are identifiable and some are not; some are within the learner's control, many are not.
- *Learning is a uniquely individualized phenomenon, a process through which everyone proceeds in unique ways and at varying rates.*

Every child who comes into our classrooms comes with a unique background shaped by varying physiological, cultural, socio-economic, and psychological and emotional factors. During their formative years these children had little to no control over these background factors, and neither did they choose the circumstances of their birth.

These background factors, in complex interplay, influence not only what a child gets to experience but the degree to which the child gets to experience those things. In turn, those experiences are what shape the child's schema (knowledge construct) (Wadsworth, 1996). Some students come into the classroom having relatively complex schemas, while others come in having relatively simple schemas.

A Key Application of Constructivist Learning Theory: Scoring vs. Grading

Given this constructivist understanding of how learning occurs, as reflective educators we can't help but contemplate some of our accepted practices ... practices such as having grade level expectations, labeling children as IEP or gifted students, having a competitive honor roll, and grading students, the focus of this article.

Whenever we grade we are using a cut-score grading scale of some kind, whether it's a letter cut-score scale (A-B-C-D-F), a number scale (4-3-2-1), or a scale of proficiency labels (Below Standard -Meets Standard-Exceeds Standard or Needs Improvement-Satisfactory-Excellent, etc.). Anytime we use a cut-score scale this automatically means we are grading students based on their level of attainment. For example, if we give a student a B what we are saying is that the student has attained a B's worth of competency or that their work is a B's worth of value. And anytime we grade students based on attainment this automatically means we are norm-referencing (comparing them to some norm).

In classrooms, students with schemas of varying complexity, whether well matched with the learning environment or not, all engage in the same general classroom experience and do so for the same duration of time. *Yet despite knowing that a) the time it takes to construct knowledge depends on the complexity of our existing schemas, and b) that complexity, in turn, affects both our readiness and availability to further construct knowledge, we routinely use norm-referenced cut-score grading scales and comparatively grade students based on their attainment within the same allotted time period (e.g., a unit, marking period, school year).*

Constructivists have helped us recognize that anytime we grade students based on attainment of a particular norm within a set time period we are automatically discriminating against a population of our students. Grading is an inherently discriminatory practice.

Rather than give grades, an alternative approach is to simply report progress scores. Standards-based, formative assessment provides an easy way for us to do this.

Getting Started with Progress Scoring

In traditional, content-based, evaluation-driven instruction students are assigned certain types of tasks, each of those tasks is graded, and then some type of weighted system and averaging are used to convert all those grades into one summative grade. In a standards-based, formative assessment approach to teaching and learning a very different process is required (Black & Wiliam, 1998;

Stiggins, 1997; Wiggins & McTighe, 1998). Instead, the approach now is to assign students a variety of different tasks, activities deliberately designed to provide multiple opportunities over time and across units of study to draw out student demonstration of a particular set of lifelong skills (standards), and then use those accumulating student pieces as evidence to help regularly measure student growth (using a progress rubric) in those standards over time.

In this approach, the student's work is not graded. The student's latest round of work (produced since the last time the student's progress rubric was marked), as a whole, is measured up against the benchmarks of progress for each criterion of the standard, the student's progress in those criteria over time is what gets reported, and that growth is reported as a score, not a grade.

For example, if our progress rubric lists ten criteria and the student, at the time of reporting, is demonstrating sustained progress in seven of those ten criteria, then the student's score is simply 7/10 or 70%. No grade is being assigned because there is no cut-score scale of any kind being used. If, however, we then decide that progress in 8-10 of the criteria equates to an A (or a 4), 6-7 earns a B, etc. we have now imposed a cut-score grading scale and have now moved from simply reporting a score to giving a grade. As we've seen, if we take that step, whether voluntarily or by mandate, not only is the grade less objective and informative than the score, it's also discriminatory. Note also how progress-based scoring not only does away with cut-score grading scales it also eliminates averaging, weighting items, composite grading (e.g., averaging test scores, homework completion, participation, etc. into one overall grade), and giving zeros ... all flawed practices that prevent us from being able to derive fair and valid grades (Marzano, 2000; Reeves, 2004).

Progress Rubrics vs. Activity-Specific Rubrics

There are two general types of rubrics ... lesson-specific rubrics and standards-based progress rubrics. Lesson-specific rubrics list criteria that are specific to the activity the students are engaging in or the task they are being asked to complete. For example, students may be asked to write an essay which then gets measured up against a rubric with criteria such as "relevant supporting details were provided," "argument was clear and concise," and "a sufficient number of examples were given." Lesson-specific rubrics are used to assess the student's work as opposed to the student's ongoing growth in skills or knowledge. Although these rubrics have a place and purpose, such as providing students guidance, they are difficult to validly and reliably translate into grades.

Standards-based progress rubrics, on the other hand, list more generalized criteria (skills) specific to the academic standards students are ultimately supposed to be assessed in. These rubrics aren't used to assess the student's work. The student's work is used as evidence to assess the student's growth in the criteria of the generalized standards being taught across content areas throughout the year.

Developing a Standards-Based Progress Rubric

What follows is a process for developing standards-based progress rubrics. In this example, we will work with two criteria, math computation and applying mathematical strategies, and the six common aspects of proficiency for which students and student work are commonly measured. Notice the two criteria are generalized and not specific to any particular task.

The first aspect of proficiency is *independence* ... can the child express the knowledge he's acquiring or perform the skill he's learning on his own without needing help, support, or prompting? In other words, has he truly internalized the knowledge or skill? Given that the standards are what we want our students to know and be able to do by the time they leave high school, independence should be measured no matter which standard or criterion is being addressed.

For each of the standards' criteria some, and in some cases perhaps all, of the remaining five aspects of proficiency that follow will also apply and therefore be important to measure.

Accuracy ... does the child perform the skill accurately? For example, it does matter how accurately a child can compute.

Relevance ... is what the child has done relevant to the task or topic at hand? For example, it matters that the child applies strategies in a relevant manner.

Because the above three aspects of proficiency are relatively definitive (i.e., the child is either doing it independently or she's not, it's either accurate or it isn't, and it's either relevant or it isn't) they can be incorporated directly into the wording of the criterion itself and do not need to be broken out into an escalating continuum of benchmarks. At this point our progress rubric looks like this:

Independently and accurately computes	
Independently and relevantly applies strategies	

The remaining three aspects of proficiency are frequency, amount, and span.

Frequency ... how often is the child able to demonstrate the skill? For example, it matters that the child can perform a basic math skill time and time again.

Amount ... how many is the child able to perform? In the case of spelling, for example, we care about how many words the child is able to spell correctly.

Span ... is the child able to demonstrate the skill across different contexts or in different situations? For example, does the child demonstrate teamwork skills no matter who she works with, and on no matter what project she is working? A second example is does the child apply her scientific method skills (observation, questioning, hypothesizing, etc.) in contexts other than science?

Unlike the first three, these three aspects of proficiency are not definitive. There are degrees of competency within which a child's performance can fall. Consequently, these aspects of proficiency do need to be broken out into a continuum that reflects growth.

Both frequency and span apply when it comes to accurate computing. It matters how often a child can compute accurately and it matters that he can do it in different contexts. Frequency, span, and amount apply to our second criterion, relevantly applies strategies. Having determined which aspects of proficiency apply to each criterion our completed progress rubric now looks like this:

Independently and accurately computes	Occasionally	Regularly	Frequently	Always (f)
	In at least one context	In a few different contexts	In several different contexts	In many different contexts (s)
Independently and relevantly applies strategies	Occasionally	Regularly	Frequently	Always (f)
	In a few different contexts	In several different contexts	In many different contexts	In every context experienced (s)
	One or two strategies	A few strategies	Several strategies	Many strategies (a)

The aspects of proficiency being measured on this rubric are independence, accuracy, relevance, frequency (f), span (s), and amount (a) and should be identified as such somewhere on the rubric (see Figure 1).

Whether these progress rubrics are common rubrics being used by multiple teachers within grade clusters or being used by individual teachers and their respective students any descriptor being used that is open to interpretation (e.g., several, occasionally, etc.) needs to be explicitly defined and those definitions, which need to be collaboratively agreed upon by everyone using the rubric, should be placed on the rubric as well (see Figure 1).

A question often asked regarding these types of descriptors is why actual numbers aren't used. With standards-based formative instruction and assessment the teacher's responsibility is to provide students with multiple opportunities in the standards over time and across contexts. The number of opportunities a teacher provides or a student receives from one classroom to the next will vary for a host of legitimate reasons. If precise numbers are used as benchmarks not only would that pose an equity problem from one classroom to the next, but could also unfairly penalize students. For example, if the fourth benchmark was set at "10 times" but the teacher was only ever able to provide her students with seven opportunities the student was never given the chance to demonstrate the skill "10 times." With fluid terms such as occasionally, regularly, and frequently no matter how many opportunities are provided from one teacher to the next these same benchmarks will still work. In the case where a student had ten opportunities and performed the skill three times, "occasionally" would describe the student's frequency of performance. For a student who had thirty opportunities and performed the skill ten times "occasionally" would describe that student's frequency as well.

In some cases an actual percentage can be valid but it depends on the nature of the criterion. For example, if the criterion is "reading accuracy," a benchmark such as "reads with 95% accuracy" would work regardless of the number of opportunities the student was given.

Marking Students on a Progress Rubric

In this example of how to use a progress rubric we will look at the first criterion of Vermont Standard 6.9: Meaning of Citizenship (VT Department of Education, 2000), which is "examines the meaning of citizenship" (see Figure 1 for complete rubric).

Meaning of Citizenship

(VT Standard 6.9)

Students examine and debate the meaning of citizenship and act as citizens in a democratic society

Independently and relevantly examines the meaning of citizenship	Occasionally	Regularly	Frequently	Always
	As it applies to a few different situations	As it applies to several different situations	As it applies to many different situations	As it applies to every situation

One of the aspects of proficiency students are periodically assessed in for this criterion is frequency. In our example we will imagine that over the past three weeks five opportunities purposefully designed to get students to "independently and relevantly examine the meaning of citizenship" have been completed by the students. These were learning opportunities intentionally embedded in a variety of different lessons/activities over the past three weeks. The teacher then decides to pause and look at one of her student's (Angel) accumulated work, all of which is being kept in the student's classroom formative assessment portfolio. Note that what qualifies as "examines" was collaboratively agreed upon ahead of time by all teachers teaching this standard and using this progress rubric, and was taught and modeled at the beginning of the year with students.

Taking a cumulative look at Angel's work the teacher sees evidence that he "independently and relevantly examined the meaning of citizenship" in three out of the five opportunities he was given. According to the collaboratively agreed upon frequency definitions listed on the rubric Angel is demonstrating this criterion on a regular basis, and so the teacher then writes the check-in date on the rubric in the box marked "regularly."

A second aspect of proficiency students are being measured in on this progress rubric is span. Because the teacher knows that one of the criteria of Standard 6.9: Meaning of Citizenship is that students be able to "independently and relevantly examine the meaning of citizenship" as it applies to multiple situations, she has deliberately embedded those first five opportunities for students into two different contexts. Not only did the students have a chance to examine the meaning of citizenship as it applies within their Social Studies unit on native culture but also as it applies to their Science unit on biodiversity.

In looking at Angel's work in these first five opportunities to engage in this standard she sees he examined the meaning of citizenship as it applied to both situations. But since application in two different situations does not yet qualify on this year-long progress rubric in the comments section at the bottom of Angel's rubric she simply writes "criterion #1 ... 2 out of 2 situations as of (that day's date)." Over the course of the year she will continue to provide multiple opportunities in additional contexts for her students to examine the meaning of citizenship. Teachers who teach one subject area will provide opportunities within each different unit they teach and, where possible, in contexts outside of their units of study.*

Assuming Standard 6.9 is a power standard (for more on power standards see Ainsworth, 2003) the teacher will continue to embed opportunities for students to work on this standard throughout the year, over time, and across units/subject areas. As work accumulates in Angel's portfolio she will periodically pause and, looking at Angel's most recent round of work as a whole (work completed since the last time his progress was recorded on his progress rubric), assess and then date his ongoing progress on this same rubric.

Perhaps two weeks and four more opportunities later the teacher again checks in on Angel's progress. Because she knew she needed to keep embedding this criterion into different contexts two of those latest opportunities were deliberately embedded into a third context, a weekly current events activity she has now instituted as part of morning meeting. In looking at Angel's work in these latest four activities, one more in Social Studies, another in Science, and two in morning meeting, she sees that he "independently and relevantly examined the meaning of citizenship" in three of the four opportunities. She also sees he not only continues to demonstrate the skill as it applies to the first two contexts, but performed it one time within a new context as well. For frequency, three out of four qualifies as "frequently" according to the definition on the rubric and because he is now demonstrating the skill in three different situations, for span he is now in the first benchmark.

Given the nature of departmentalized teaching, subject area teachers might have to look at all of the student's work, not just the student's latest round of work when measuring span.

From Progress Rubric to Progress-Based Report Card

Below is a sample portion of what a standards-based, progress-based, criterion-referenced report card might look like. Despite the discriminatory nature of grades and grading there remains demand for norm-referenced, attainment-based information. The "attainment score" on this report card meets that demand without having to resort to grades (see explanation below). However, to reiterate the key point of this article one last time, if Angel had been graded the grades he would have received have been inserted off to the side of the report card. Looking at both sets of information, which of the four forms of reporting – progress score, attainment score, progress grade, attainment grade – is a) most likely to motivate students, b) most informative, c) most objective, d) most fair, and e) least discriminatory?

Student:	Angel			Date: December 20, 2008
Semester:	Fall			
Standard	Progress Score	Attainment Score	Grade P	Grade A
Meaning of Citizenship	5/6	1/6	A	D
Examines meaning of citizenship	2/2	1/2		
Debates meaning of citizenship	2/2	0/2		
Acts as a citizen	1/2	0/2		

The remaining power standards would be listed down the left hand column.

Meaning of Citizenship is one of the power standards in which student progress is being reported. The report card lists below this standard its three criteria which are found on the VT Standard 6.9: Meaning of Citizenship progress rubric (see Figure 1). There are two aspects of proficiency being measured for each of the three criteria (see rubric), hence the denominator 2 for each criterion. Consequently, there are a total of six aspects of proficiency for this standard as a whole. The standard and its three criteria are copied right from the progress rubric for this standard, which students and parents would be familiar with prior to receiving this progress report/report card.

The "Progress Score" is the number of the standard's criteria in which the student is demonstrating sustained progress at the time of reporting (in Angel's case, 5 out of 6), which the student's most recently filled out progress rubric and accompanying work in the student's classroom formative assessment portfolio would evidence.

The "Attainment Score" is the number of the standard's criteria for which the student has reached the third benchmark of progress on the progress rubric at the time of reporting (in Angel's case, 1 out of 6), which the student's most recently completed progress rubric and accompanying work in the student's portfolio would show.

The "Grade" that has been added to the report solely for the purpose of this discussion is a norm-referenced, comparative measure of worth based on where the student's performance falls on an arbitrarily decided (as they all are) cut-score grading scale. In this example the collaboratively agreed upon scale for all power standards with six criteria is 5-6 = A, 4 = B, 3 = C, 1-2 = D, 0 = F.

"Grade P" is the progress grade (Angel got an A) and "Grade A" is the attainment grade (Angel got a D).

At the bottom of the report card would be a comments section for observations such as the following:

> Angel showed some nice growth in his ability to debate the meaning of citizenship since progress report time in October, going from just showing progress in frequency to showing progress in both frequency and span, but regressed in span for acts of citizenship. When I asked him about it he said his reason was because he was frustrated he was still being graded by some of his teachers but realizes now that not being a good citizen was not the right way to protest.

Going back to the five questions in the first paragraph of this section, when we look at Angel's report card, consider the constructivist proposition put forth in this article, and take into account the beneficial effects formative assessment has on students (Black & Wiliam, 1998), arguably the one form of reporting that is most accountable to all five questions is **progress scores.**

Conclusion

There is a glaring disconnect between what we know about learners and learning, and grading. There is a gaping disconnect between the day-to-day standards-based formative instruction and assessment now occurring in classrooms, and the traditional grading that students are still being subjected to. As with any change, there are many reasons why we have been slow to recognize and respond to these mismatches. Implementing the shifts in thinking and practice listed in Table 1 will help in our quest to rectify the way we report student learning. Three shifts in particular that will expedite this needed transformation are 1) recognizing and accepting that grading students based on attainment of developmental norms within "one-time-fits-all" time periods such as units and marking periods is an inherently discriminatory process, 2) turning our focus from attainment to progress, and 3) adopting the use of progress rubrics (as opposed to just activity-specific rubrics) and switching from giving grades to simply reporting scores

Figure 1: Progress Rubric

Name: _____Dates_____

Meaning of Citizenship
(VT Standard 6.9)

Students examine and debate the meaning of citizenship and act as citizens in a democratic society

Independently and relevantly examines the meaning of citizenship*	Occasionally	Regularly	Frequently	Always
	As it applies to a few different situations	As it applies to several different situations	As it applies to many different situations	As it applies to every situation
Independently and relevantly debates the meaning of citizenship*	Within a few different contexts	Within several different contexts	Within many different contexts	Within every context
Independently acts a citizen*	Regularly	Frequently	Always	Publicly known exemplar
	In several different situations	In many different situations	In every situation	Publicly known exemplar

*See student portfolio for evidence   Aspects of Proficiency = independence, relevance, frequency, span

Additional Comments/Observations:

Bibliography

Ainsworth, L. (2003). *Power standards: Identifying the standards that matter the most.* Englewood, CO: Advanced Learning Press.

Black, P. & Wiliam, D. (1998). Inside the black box: Raising standards through classroom assessment. *Phi Delta Kappan,* October, 1998.

Brooks, J. G. & Brooks, M. G. (1993). *In search of understanding: A case for constructivist classrooms.* Alexandria, VA: ASCD.

Caine, R. N. & Caine, G. (1994*). Making connections: Teaching and the human brain.* New York, NY: Addison-Wesley.

Dunn, K., Scileppi, J., Averna, L., Zerillo, V., & Skelding, M. (2007). *The contemporary application of a systems approach to education: Models for effective reform.* (Chapter 3). Lanham, MD: University Press of America.

Guskey, T. R. (1994). Making the grade: What benefits students? *Educational Leadership,* 52 (2): 14-20.

Herman, J. L., Aschbacher, P. R., & Winters, L. (1992*). A practical guide to alternative assessment.* Alexandria, VA: ASCD.

Kohn, A. (1996). *Punished by rewards.* New York, NY: Houghton-Mifflin.

Marzano, R. J. (2006). *Classroom assessment & grading that work.* Alexandria, VA: ASCD.

___. (2000). *Transforming classroom grading.* Alexandria, VA: ASCD.

Reeves, D. B. (2004). The case against the zero. *Phi Delta Kappan,* 86 (4): 324-325.

Skelding, M. (2008*). Lasting results: Rediscovering the promise of standards through assessment-based instruction.* Montpelier, VT: Common Roots Press.

Stiggins, R. J. (1997). *Student-centered classroom assessment.* Upper Saddle, NJ: Prentice Hall.

Vermont Department of Education. (2000*). Vermont framework of standards and learning opportunities.* Montpelier, VT: Vermont Department of Education.

Wadsworth, B. J. (1996). *Piaget's theory of cognitive and affective development*. White Plains, NY: Longman.

Wiggins, G. & McTighe, J. (1998). *Understanding by design*. Alexandria, VA: ASCD.

Noteworthy contemporaries whose work deserves mentioning include Susan M. Brookhart, Ginette Delandshere, Peter Johnston, Gary Natriello, and Rick Wormeli.

Let's Put Yourselves in Your Students' Shoes

The approach to standards-based formative instruction and assessment, grading, and reporting that we've been exploring in this course has been challenging to fully grasp, and perhaps fully accept ... and for legitimate and understandable reasons. And what's regulating that for us is the constructivist learning principles that govern all of us in terms of our readiness and availability to assimilate, accommodate, and construct new knowledge and understanding.

Sometimes, when we're experiencing dissonance, if we try to suspend ourselves from our own bounds and place ourselves within the bounds of others (in this case, our students) we can better assimilate/accommodate the dissonance we feel when we encounter new information, ideas, and experiences. So with that in mind here's one more attempt to help us take another, perhaps new, look at this approach to grading.

Let's start with our own realities. Each one of you is a teacher, and each of you has X number of students you're responsible for. Being the teacher, you have a set of standards/goals/objectives/outcomes/norms/criteria – whatever you want to call them – you desire every one of your students to meet. The standards to which you are holding your students dictate the grades they receive from you. Performance at what you consider is A level work is the standard you ultimately want every student to achieve.

Your students come into your classroom with schemas of varying degrees of complexity and in different configurations and states of construction. In other words, the students in your class are not all on the same level playing field cognitively, not to mention emotionally or philosophically.

Each one of those students will experience the same basic instruction from you, and will have the same basic amount of exposure to your instruction (e.g., length of class time, a unit, a marking period). And, as happens every marking period, you will have some students who will meet your A level expectations within the allotted time frame and some who will not. Because we know they all didn't start out cognitively on the same level playing field we know that the reason some won't meet your A level expectations isn't simply because they are less intelligent or less motivated than those who will. With more time and some differentiated accommodation to their existing schemas and learning styles they, too, could eventually meet that expectation. But schools work on inflexible time schedules, students don't get differentiated time frames in which to learn, and they get comparatively ranked against each other using one-time-fits-all time frames for learning and one-scale-fits-all cut-score grading scales.

So now let's be our students. I'll be the teacher and you will be my students. If I were using the traditional approach I would have an ultimate expectation I would hope each of you would attain by the end of the course, and that level of performance would equate to A level work.

That A level work, in this case, would be that by the end of our May session you would understand and be able to state the reasons why traditional grading practices are invalid, unreliable, and inherently discriminatory. You would also be demonstrating tangible evidence in your classroom that you are effectively transitioning your practice from unit-based instruction to standards-based instruction, and from reporting student learning using norm-referenced grading to reporting their learning using criterion-referenced scoring. And, it would be clear that your students understood why that transition was occurring. Those would have been my criteria for earning an A in this course.

But who the heck am I!? What right is it of mine, alone, to hold you to my biased idea of what qualifies as A work and, even more audacious than that, then be the one to ultimately judge (grade) your learning? By doing so I would ultimately regulate your opportunities in life (like the grades we are giving our students are doing for and to them) by comparing your rate of learning to that of your classmates over the span of our nine weeks together (a one-time-fits-all time frame). Sorry for ranting. Back to you being in your students' shoes.

Each one of you came into this course with schemas of varying degrees of complexity and in different configurations and states of construction. Each one of you has different historical (your background, experiential base, and world view) and logistical (your current teaching assignment) variables influencing and regulating your availability, readiness, and ability to construct meaning from what you're experiencing in this course.

Each one of you sat through the same instruction from the same teacher (remember, there's no way I, or any teacher, can be equally responsive to all your different "histories" because I'm enveloped in my own unique "history"), you all had the same amount of time interacting with that instruction, and you will all eventually be given a grade at the same time (at the end of a one-time-fits-all time frame for learning).

Since I would not be using the bell curve (now taboo) it wouldn't appear that I was overtly comparing you to one another. *However, when I use any form of cut-score grading scale I am still comparing you to one another.* If I use a cut-score scale I am comparing you against each other relative to your schema coming into the class and how fast or slow you are able to learn the material relative to others. Our tendency is to attribute low grades to lack of effort or motivation but there's a complex of factors that regulates how quickly one learns.

And now to the final point ... If this theoretical example were reality, unless I lowered my standard of what qualifies as A work (which, when we do that we really expose the fallacy of grades, what they actually reflect, and how invalid a measure they are) I would not be able to give any of you an A by course's end.

As you just read that did you have an immediate reaction of "that's ridiculous" or "your standard is too high" or "it would not be fair for you to try to grade us after so little time?" Did you feel offended or some other form of anger, frustration, or disbelief? And did you immediately attribute you not getting an A to me, my methodology, my personality, my opinions and the way in which I shared them, the once-a-month structure of this course, the logistics of your teaching situation, not having adequate time to apply what you've been learning, the legitimacy (or lack of) of the topic, the prohibitive constraints of the system you work in, lack of support from your administrators, etc., etc., etc.?

Those objections are similar to the ones our students regularly express over their grades and being graded. *And if you did object you would absolutely be justified in doing so! But not for those reasons I listed. They are simply examples of contextual elements that naturally influence and regulate each of our abilities to construct knowledge.* **They are the given, not the problem. Grading is the problem.**

With the approach we've been exploring in this course the above scenario and reactions would and could never occur. Students are never compared to one another through use of cut-score grading scales, and therefore never unfairly rewarded or punished because of pre-existing conditions or the way in which differentiated learning naturally occurs from one individual to the next. In this approach student learning is scored rather than graded and that score is based on the progress they make in accordance with their natural and unique learning curves.

Why Are We Still Grading Students?

We have sound theories helping us see why grading is illogical. We have uncovered how the mechanics of grading are technically flawed. We have known for some time now that inequities exist among learners, the very inequities that give us ethical justification for doing away with comparative norm-referenced grading. And, there exist valid, reliable, and fair alternatives to reporting student learning that positively motivate and don't discriminate against and cull children.

Yet we continue to embrace grading! Why are we still grading students? A quick look at theoretical, technical, and ethical issues around grading will help as we self-reflect on this question.

Systems theory explains that all things are in a constant state of transformation and evolution. Nothing is static, and there is no finality to anything. Everything continually shapes and is continually shaped by the things they are in constant interaction with. In other words, all things exist within interdependencies that are formative.

Constructivist theory reveals that learning is no exception. It, too, is a formative process, not summative. Our knowledge is in a continual state of construction, deconstruction, and reconstruction, and with every experience or interaction we have, our schemas evolve. Our knowledge is never static.

Accordingly, we use formative assessment to monitor our students' ongoing progress and schema development. *But grading is antithetical to that.* It is an attempt to total up, assign a fixed value to, and then categorize within a cut-score grading scale the learner's knowledge construct at given points in time. The two theories just mentioned clearly reveal the illogicality of grading (summative evaluation). *By the time the grade is assigned it's already obsolete.* Yet we use those obsolete misrepresentations of what a student knows and is able to do to both define him and regulate his opportunities for success.

If the fact that grades are instantly obsolete isn't enough to convince us of the fallacy of grading, perhaps the technical flaws within the mechanics of grading will. Those flaws include averaging, weighting, composite grading, and giving zeros.

With averaging, even if the grades we use were valid, when we average we take our most current measure of student learning and combine it with a number of older measures ... grades that presumably reflected the student's knowledge construct at earlier stages of development. Consequently, an average, at best, is a measure of where a student's learning was at some point in the past. Furthermore, trying to report student *progress* using a method that is naturally *regressive* (the impact each subsequent grade has on the overall average lessens as grades accumulate) is curious.

Weighting is not only an arbitrary and subjective practice, it automatically discriminates against certain learning styles. For example, if tests are worth 60%, homework 30%, and class participation 10%, not only are certain learning styles being favored, but certain backgrounds and home situations (e.g., equity issues around homework) as well.

The same is true of composite grading, which typically incorporates averaging and weighting. When we combine grades received in different skill sets such as test scores (knowledge acquisition), homework completion (responsibility, time management), class participation (intersocial skills), and effort (motivation, perseverance) into one grade, we again discriminate against learning styles and we assign a grade that leaves stakeholders having to guess or presume which of those skills the child actually possesses, and to what degree.

Like averaging, giving zeros is mathematically flawed and unfair, and can also be an equity issue if the zeros are for incomplete homework. Speaking mathematically, the numerical gaps between 100, 90, 80, 70, and 60 are ten points but between 59 and 0 is fifty nine points. Any measure of student learning that includes zeros averaged in is obviously invalid, not to mention that a zero is rarely a measure of learning but rather punishment for incomplete work.

As we've seen, there are theoretical and technical reasons why grading should be abandoned. There are ethical issues as well. *Constructivist theory not only reveals that grading is illogical, but that it is also blatantly discriminatory.* We now understand that interaction and experiences are what stimulate connections within our brains, which in turn further knowledge construction and schema development. We also know that a child's background is a complex mix of interacting physical, psychological, social, and cultural factors, for which no two children are the same. And those factors, most of which the child has no control over, regulate not only what the child gets to experience but to what degree she gets to experience it.

No two children enter our classrooms on a level playing field. Their schemas are as different as their fingerprints. Consequently, our students can't possibly experience any single lesson or activity in the same way, or learn the material at the same rate. *Because typical school design severely limits our ability to truly differentiate our instruction, and grading continues to be done in one-size-fits-all time periods – the length of a unit, marking period, school year – grading is a discriminatory practice.*

As we can see, we have more than enough logic and rationale for ending the practice of grading. But given that it is emotion that regulates intellect, it is not surprising that emotion can easily override logic. *What emotion could possibly allow us to willfully dismiss what we know about grading and consciously choose to continue the practice?*

Some argue we grade because it's mandated by school policy. Others blame it on indifference. Teachers just don't feel that grading is a battle worth fighting. Still others attribute it to acquiescence. Transforming grading is simply too monumental a task for teachers at their level in the larger system to take on. And some say we grade because we've never known anything different. *But again, the question is not why we grade but why, now that we've exposed grading for what it really is, we continue to grade.* Teachers who are student-centered and know, or at least hear discourse on the dark side of grading, would not let contrary policy, indifference, acquiescence, or ignorance serve as excuses to continue grading. There must be something deeper and more insidious at work.

Although the list of human emotions is quite long and varied, there is only a handful that could sway us to consciously choose to do something despite overwhelming evidence not to. We just looked at two of those emotions, apathy (indifference) and discouragement (acquiescence). But again, we are child advocates or we wouldn't be in education. We would not succumb to either of these emotions at the expense of our students.

Another emotion that can influence us to do something we know we shouldn't is anger. Take crime and self-destructive behavior as examples. Yet it's hard to picture this emotion being the one behind why we continue to grade students. Who or what could we be angry at that our anger would manifest itself in this way? The students? Our mothers?

If it's not apathy, discouragement, or anger perhaps it's pride? Could having graded students for so long only to discover that we'd been imposing a flawed practice on children all those years embarrass or shame us so badly that we would choose denial over change? Or could uncovering the dubious nature of grading, a practice that afforded us so much of our own self-worth, self-identity, and opportunities in life be so disturbing that it feels better to just stand by the practice? But progressive teachers understand the phenomenological nature of teaching and learning. They understand that it is a continually evolving "science" and that what was once considered cutting edge practice is more often than not eventually exposed as anything but ... and that is simply the nature of teaching and learning. Yes, it pains us to know we could have done better for our past students but upon learning that we do whatever it takes to do better for our current students.

Although pride might be a possibility the emotion we can most likely attribute to our resistance to stand up against grading is fear. Why are we still grading students? Because we are afraid not to and to change feels threatening. And that fear has many layers. One we just discussed. If it is pride at work, pride is simply a form of denial and denial is simply fear in disguise. If we are too proud to admit an accept the fallacy of grading, or are in some other way denying there are problems with grading, we are simply exhibiting fear.

Fear can be at play on a more superficial level as well. For some of us there might be fear of conflict. Changing something as culturally entrenched as grading can be highly contentious, and in this case especially challenging given the number of stakeholders who still accept the practice. For others of us perhaps it's fear of risk. Grading is taken for granted by most to be a valid practice. A new way of reporting student learning will be untested. What if it doesn't work? Or what if people don't like it? And for some of us it might be fear of change. A new approach is unfamiliar and will require new learning and effort on our part. It's also a perturbation that causes discomfort and insecurity. It's easier and more comfortable to stick with the familiar, and in the case of grading, much more comfortable given the risk and conflict involved in trying to change it.

Regardless of which fear we identify as ours, not one of them is student-centered.

Fear did not keep us from entering the high stakes field of education. Why then do we continue to let fear keep us from changing a practice within our practice that is so arguably wrong? The realities of grading have been exposed and transformation of grading practices is painfully overdue. It is time to stop grading students and instead simply report which skills they are demonstrating sustained progress in and which they are not.

A Feel for What Your Child is Experiencing with Grades and Grading

After sitting through a period of instruction we gave parents in attendance a short, 14 item quiz on the material that had been presented. We then corrected their quizzes and explained to them that we could have determined their grades using one of three types of cut-score grading scales. The first was a differentiated scale pre-determined by the teacher. That scale was 12-14=A, 10-11=B, 8-9=C, 6-7=D, 0-5=F.

We also explained that we could have simply used the traditional 90-100=A, 80-89=B, etc. cut-score scale. And finally, we explained that we could have looked at the distribution of their scores and drew lines dividing the range of scores into five groups, A's-F's.

After they had a chance to see where they fell on those three different grading scales and discussing with them the validity issue with just the fact that three different types of cut-score grading scales are being randomly and subjectively used by teachers, we then presented the following point.

As happens with your children in their classrooms, you all sat through the same "instruction." You all had the same teachers, were provided the same materials, had the exact same amount of time to learn what was being taught, and were all judged on the same norms. Yet what resulted was a wide range of scores. When we applied those scores to a cut-score grading scale some of you got better grades than others. Some of you got A's and the rest of you didn't. Although we all know grades mean different things from different teachers, the one common assumption about grades is they identify who is and isn't "smart." How many of you truly believe that those of you who got A's are "smarter" than those who didn't? Said differently, do those of you who did not get an A agree that you are less intelligent than those who did get A's? We know there are a multitude of factors behind why some of you got A's this time and the rest of you didn't ... factors many of which you had/have no control over, and many of which have nothing to do with who is "smarter" or "better" than who (remember the "Trees Diagram" {see Section Three})

The other reality about grades is despite the fact that we all know they mean different things from different teachers, and that they and the lines drawn between them are extremely subjective, grades are final, official, and they never go away. Grades categorize and define our children and that, in turn, regulates our children's opportunities in life. "Smart" students get to select their opportunities in life. Those not deemed "smart" get select opportunities.

This discussion over measuring our students' progress/growth as opposed to grading them ultimately comes down to what our beliefs are about children, learning, and school. Do we believe school should be a place where every child learns and experiences success? Or do we believe the role of school is to select ... to sort, rank, and cull our children? Traditional grading serves the latter, standards-based progress scoring serves the former.

And so to turn your quiz into an example of what a standards-based approach would look like. Each of the 14 questions on the quiz would actually be 14 criteria from the Vermont Standards. The score you got, let's say 5/14, would be an *initial* (as opposed to *final*) measurement of your competency in those 14 criteria.

Throughout the year your teacher would continue to give you multiple opportunities of varying kinds throughout different units of study to help you continue to expand your competency in those 14 criteria. Periodically, you and your teacher would check in, look at the most recent work you've done, and measure the gains you've made since the last time you were assessed. Perhaps the second time you're assessed your work showed that you had made gains (progressed) in 7 of the 14 criteria. And at report card time you were up to 8 out of 14.

In this approach 8/14 is what would appear on your report card, indicating that during the marking period you demonstrated continued growth in 8 out of the 14 criteria, more than half your criteria. Your traditional grade in this case would be a C- (actually an F+ if the 90-100=A, etc. grading scale were used).

Would those of you who got a grade of C- but wanted an A be any less motivated than if you got a score of 8/14 but wanted a 14/14? Asked another way, would those of you who got an 8/14 be less or more inspired than if you had received a C-? And which of the two would be more informative and more accurately reflect how much learning you did during the marking period.

If It Looks Like A Duck, ...

We hear so much these days about transformation in education, including how we now grade students. But look closely at those so-called changes in grading. The way we measure and report student learning remains a sham and far from "markedly changed in form or appearance."

Since the 1980's two of our widely read education journals, *Educational Leadership* and *Phi Delta Kappan*, have regularly devoted entire issues to the subjects of assessment and grading. Articles by select leaders in the field appear regularly in both periodicals, and each of these authors has done extraordinary work helping us understand and apply formative assessment.

Their work has also pushed us to reflect on how we grade students. *Unfortunately, it stops short of genuinely dealing with grading.* As sound and vital as standards-based formative instruction and assessment is, it does not legitimize grading. In fact, the two are incompatible. And the harder we try to institute formative assessment, and still hold on to grading, the further we expose grading for the sham that it is.

Why a sham? The answer starts with theory. Systems theory explains that all things are formative, continually shaping and being shaped by the things with which they interact. There is no finality to anything.

Constructivist theory reveals that learning is no exception. Our knowledge is in a continual state of construction, deconstruction, and reconstruction because with every interaction we have our schemas evolve. Our knowledge is never static.

Accordingly, we use formative assessment to monitor our students' learning. *But grading is antithetical to that.* It is an attempt to assign a fixed value to a student's ever changing schema. The two theories just mentioned reveal how illogical that is. *By the time a grade is assigned it's already obsolete.* This is especially alarming given how grades define students and, in turn, regulate their opportunities in life.

A third theory, phenomenology, is indicting as well. It explains that every object we interact with or event we experience we subjectively define relative to our unique life experience. The personal meaning that a student's work has to a teacher the moment she grades it, combined with the context in which she grades it, influences the grade she gives. This subjectivity is natural and unavoidable but that doesn't let grading off the hook. *Subjectivity should be a reason to abandon grading, not acquiesce to it.* For more on this discussion please see my article, "Color Blindness and Grading," *Education Week* online commentary, February 11, 2011.

Aside from these theoretical indictments, grading also has serious technical flaws. These include averaging, weighting, composite grading, and giving zeros, all of which were addressed in that same commentary. To add to that conversation on averaging I'll use baseball as an analogy. How hitters do at the start of the season has a disproportionate impact on their overall average because the impact that each subsequent at-bat has on their evolving average incrementally lessens over time. This is especially sad for those whose bats "come alive" later in the season. In essence, slow starting hitters are punished for not starting out with a 1.000 batting average. Likewise, averaging punishes "late blooming" students. For that matter, it punishes any student on a natural learning curve ... which is every student.

In addition, variables such as the different number of total at-bats each hitter gets, the batters and/or pitchers alternately getting better with more practice or worse due to fatigue, the particular pitchers a batter faces and how often they face them, and a host of other variables all affect a hitter's average. Is the hitter with the highest batting average at the end of the season truly the best hitter? Is the student with the highest average at report card time truly the best at whatever that grade purportedly reflects?

And these are simply the technical flaws of averaging. What's most disturbing about averaging student grades is that it involves taking our most current measure of student learning and diluting it with grades the student received when his schema was less developed. But each new experience the student had after receiving those earlier grades both changed and expanded the student's overall schema.

As if we need more reasons to do away with grading, the "final nail in grading's coffin" is that it is blatantly discriminatory. The backgrounds children come from regulate not only what they get to experience but the degree to which they get to experience it. Those backgrounds are what shape each of their schemas and their schemas are as different as their fingerprints. Consequently, they can't possibly experience a lesson in the same way, or learn the material at the same rate. Yet we continue to grade them within one-size-fits-all time periods – the length of a unit, marking period, school year.

For this last point let's turn to baseball again. Like grade levels and marking periods nine innings is an arbitrary time span. The team that has the most runs after nine innings is deemed the winner, and with winning comes numerous privileges and assumptions about the quality of the team. But is the winning team truly the better team? The losing team in that contest might have had more runs through 8 ½ innings and, had the game gone beyond nine innings, might have regained and then held the lead on into infinity. A student who receives a D at report card time, with more time and additional experiences could get an A. So is she an A student or a D student?

It's assumed that if teachers are conducting standards-based formative instruction and assessment grading must therefore be criterion-referenced (as opposed to norm-referenced) and therefore simply incidental to the assessment process. But this is false. *Grades are still being derived through flawed practices and grading students within one-size-fits-all time periods is the most unethical comparative norm we could possibly use.*

Students and parents have the right to question why we continue to grade students. *In fact, they should be outraged.* Fear of change, fear of risk in trying something new, and fear of conflict we'll face trying to change it are no excuse for sticking with grading. Burying ourselves in denial because it's too hard to acknowledge all those years we engaged in grading, or too hard to accept that grades unfairly played a major role in our own success at the expense of others is wrong as well. And claiming we have no choice but to give grades because of the computerized grade books and report cards we've adopted is like saying we have to consume because stores accommodate our demand for goods.

Have we really transformed grading? Or are we once again simply conforming to it? If we are serious about transforming grading then let's give formative assessment an honest try. Let's stop grading students and instead simply measure and report how much progress each is sustaining in the standards. Then we'll be able to say with a straight face that we have truly transformed grading and that students are no longer "falling through the (same old) 'quacks'."

Averaging and Cut-Score Grading Scales

In addition to technical quality issues (validity, reliability, fairness), common evaluation strategies such as averaging a student's scores or grades and the use of cut-score grading scales are coming under question as well (Marzano, 2000). In the case of averaging, for example, when a student's scores or grades are averaged the result is actually a misrepresentation of how much true learning the student has done. The only way averaging works is if all variables remain fixed from the first score to the last. However, with teaching and learning and child development fixed variables are virtually impossible because they, their interplay, and their interaction with external influences are never static or predictable. They are fluid.

Cut-scores are the lines drawn that separate one level of proficiency from another. For example, a traditional cut-score grading scale commonly used by teachers is 90-100=A, 80-89=B, etc. Although this approach generally allows for ease and convenience in determining and reporting grades, it can easily be argued that it is of poor technical quality for several reasons.

First, the drawing of these lines and designation of grades therein was and is an arbitrary and subjective practice. Second, this

approach neither accounts for the variability in the number of criteria on which the evaluation is based nor the degree of difficulty
of each item being scored. For example, a two out of three (2/3) on
an essay test equates to the same grade (D) as 66 out of 100 on a
multiple choice test. Although the grades are comparable the performances are not. Since the number of criteria in the first evaluation is only three, the final quantification of that performance
does not reflect its qualitative value. Not only is achieving two out
of three commendable in most real world contexts, in this case it
was two out of three tasks that required higher order thinking skills
than did the multiple choice test. As Doran (2003) argued, a final fallacy with cut-score categories is they are gross measures that fail to
recognize growth students are making within a particular cut-score
category.

Doran, H. C. (2003). Adding value to accountability. *Educational
Leadership* 61 (3), 57.

Marzano, R. J. (2000). *Transforming classroom grading.* Alexandria,
VA: ASCD.

Baseball, Grades, and Averaging

Just one of the many lessons that baseball teaches us about all
kinds of things ...

It can be argued that batting averages are invalid and unfair reflections of a hitter's ability. They reflect neither the hitter's overall
general ability nor the hitter's actual proficiency at the time of reporting.

How hitters do at the start of the season has a disproportionate
impact on their evolving average. The impact each subsequent at
bat has on the overall average is regressive (incrementally lessens
over time). If batters "get hot" later in the season (i.e., the "A students" at that time and in that context) not only will their average not reflect their proficiency at that time, but the impact that
these "late bloomers'" progress has on their overall average is pro-

gressively less the later in the season they "bloom." In essence, late
bloomers are punished for not starting out at the A level norm.

In addition, variables such as the different number of total at
bats each hitter gets, the batters and/or pitchers alternately getting
better with more practice or worse due to fatigue over the course
of the season, the particular pitchers a batter faces and how often
they face them, etc., etc., etc. all affect a hitter's average.

Is the batter with the highest average at the end of the season
truly the best hitter? Is the batter's average a true reflection of her
progress? What about her potential? Aren't progress and potential what we say we value and want to focus on most with every
student? Can we see the discrimination inherent in averaging and
grading based on attainment of developmental norms, and in using
averages and grades in a norm-referenced way?

Rainfall Averages vs. Grade Averages

An annual rainfall average is simply the total amount of rain that
fell over X number of years divided by X. For example, if 100 inches
of rain fell over the last ten years, if we evenly divvied up the 100
inches of rain across those ten years the result would suggest that
"on average" it rained ten inches each year ... even if, in fact, from
year 1-9 it rained a total of 45 inches (maybe five inches each year,
maybe not) and during year ten alone it rained 55 inches. The average serves as an approximation (a potentially misleading one as
our example shows) of how much rain fell each year and it serves as
an estimate (a potentially poor one as our example shows) of how
much rain will fall next year ... and only for that next year because
that year's total will again change the overall average.

This rainfall example shows that even when we try to rely on
averages with things that are *not* in a continuous state of growth
those averages have very limited validity, reliability, and predictive
value.

As we know from cognitive science and constructivist learning
knowledge construction *is* in a continuous state of growth. It is a

formative process, continually shaping and being shaped by experience. It is never static, and there is never any finality to learning. It is a fluid, continually evolving work-in-progress.

If rainfall did steadily build like our knowledge constructs do, would there be any value in trying to determine average annual rainfall? If we did try, the average *might* coincidentally be the amount that fell during one of those years being averaged in, but could only be correct for just that one year. And in terms of predictive value we would already know that even our most recent average (if we were able to reliably determine it) is going to be below the actual amount of rainfall that we are inevitably going to receive that next year. And because of the many variables that regulate rainfall we would have no way of knowing just how far below. The validity, reliability, and predictive value of an average for something that is ever increasing are virtually zero.

In the above example we pretended that rainfall steadily increases over time. With learning we don't have to pretend. Knowledge construction does steadily increase over time.

Baseball, Grades, and Cut-Scores

Yet one more of those many lessons baseball teaches us about all kinds of things ...

Nine innings is essentially an arbitrary "cut-score." The team with the most runs at the end of nine innings is deemed the "winner," and with winning comes numerous privileges and assumptions about the quality of that team. But is the winning team the better team? The so-called "loser" might have had more runs through 8 ½ inning and, had the game gone beyond nine innings might have regained and then held the lead on into infinity.

A student who receives a D at report card time, with more time and additional experiences could get an A. So is he an A student or a D student?

What cut-score grading scales actually do is rank students according to their readiness to learn, and readiness is regulated by a complex of background and experience variables, most of which students have no control over.

What purpose does it serve to score student work and then take those scores and plug them into a pre- or post-determined common cut-score scale (e.g., 40-50=A, 30-39=B, etc.) and convert their scores into grades? Although the range of grades we would end up with might suggest who knows more than who at that moment in time (just their scores would do that, too), there are many legitimate experience/background related reasons why each student is at a different stage in their knowledge of the topic being taught. Why honor and reward students with advanced knowledge by giving them a high grade, and shame and punish those with less knowledge by giving them a low grade?

And, as we regularly check in and assess our students' growing knowledge we might find that those students who knew the least at given points now know the most. And there will be legitimate reasons why those who knew the least now know the most and vice versa.

So what purpose do any preceding grades serve ... which of course prompts the question, "Well, then what purpose do any grades serve?"

Constructivist Learning vs. "One-Time-Frame-Fits-All" Grading

We know that the backgrounds (cultural, socio-economic, physiological, psychological) and cumulative experience each of our students comes to class with vary widely. They are as different as each of their fingerprints. We also know that background and experience are what shapes an individual's schema/cognitive framework/knowledge construct/world view/gestalt. And we know each one of those is as different from one student to the next as their fingerprints are ... and toe prints as well?

Background and experience also influence a student's readiness and/or availability to learn. In short, students entering our classrooms are not all on the same level playing field. They are not all on the same starting line. *And they are not all on the same starting line for valid, legitimate, credible reasons most of which the student had no control over.*

With grading systems such as Beyond Standard-At Standard-Below Standard what we are doing is setting a **timed norm**. After a set period of time (end of a unit, marking period, school year) every student is comparatively judged and categorized as to whether or not they have "met the standard" (or are performing at an A level or a 3 level) within the same one-time-fits-all allotted time for learning.

For those students who "meet the standard" assumptions are made about them as learners and specific privileges are bestowed upon them accordingly ... assumptions and consequences that are very different than for those who do not "meet the standard" within that same time period. In essence, the students who come into the classroom further from the timed norm that we have set generally end up being relatively punished, and those who come in closer to the timed norm generally end up being relatively rewarded ... even though we know that there are legitimate, beyond-their-control factors behind why some of our students have a head start toward our timed norms.

To supplement and complement this big picture view of constructivist learning and grading let's consider a small picture example ... our students who have to miss school for some reason. As hard as we may try it's fair to say that when a student misses class time (the teacher's face-to-face interactive instruction, the accompanying class discussion, the social learning that occurs during accompanying cooperative group work) what they miss can never fully be made up or replaced. Essentially, every time they miss class they have lost ground to others in what is basically a race toward the timed norm we've set (Meets the Standard; A; 3) against which we ultimately comparatively judge every one of our students.

Grading is clearly an ethical, social justice, equity issue we can no longer deny or avoid confronting.

Allotted Time for Learning

Regardless of all the different ways we teach, assess, and grade our students the one universal norm against which every one of us is comparatively norming our kids, despite knowing they've had unequal accessibility to learning, have varying levels of readiness to learn, and varying levels of availability for learning, is our *one-time-allotment-to-learn-fits-all* grading periods ... the length of a unit, marking period, and school year.

Your Peer Conferences and the Disconnect Between Constructivist Learning and Grading

After just two or three peer conferences (as well as our whole group discussions and your small group discussions) I'm willing to bet that you are seeing that your classmates are all in very different places with respect to their knowledge, understanding, and application of the content and skills we're exploring in this course ... even though they have all received the same information and participated in the same learning opportunities from the same instructor over the same amount of class time. Why is that?

Different levels of readiness

They are all starting out with different degrees of related experience and backgrounds ... something they can't erase, for the most part had no control over, and are not at fault for not having the ability to predict that one day they would be in this context and should've made the appropriate life choices that would have set them up to be on par or ahead of the game in this work.

Different levels of availability for learning

Their different world views and emotional associations are influencing how much and how quickly they can accommodate and assimilate this information. The more dissonance the material is causing for them, the harder and slower that accommodation and assimilation. How perturbing it is depends on how contrary the material is to their overall schema and gestalt, both of which have been shaped by their life experience, much of which (childhood) they had no control over.

Different levels of access to learning

Their different personal circumstances are influencing how much time and effort they can put into internalizing the information from this course. As well, their different professional circumstances are influencing how much of that information they are able to actually apply (and thereby further learn by doing) in their classroom toward their course project. They can only work with what they have to work with.

Knowing all of this, would it be valid and fair to grade all of you, keeping in mind that grading means comparatively ranking the worth of your work (which, whether we like to admit it or not most stakeholders translate into a judgment of you) through use of a common cut-score grading scale ... and grade you all at the same time (i.e., within the same time frame; after the same amount of learning time)? Wouldn't we simply be trying to compare apples and oranges ... and grapes ... and lemons ... and grapefruits ... and limes ... and ...?

Disconnect Continued

Contrary to the belief that grades are a reflection of our students' intelligence and proficiency they are actually a comparative measure of our students' readiness for learning, availability to learn, access to learning, and willingness to comply. All four of these factors are regulated by a complex of background and experience variables, most of which our students have no control over. This is why grading (comparative evaluation) is a discriminatory practice.

Let's look at you guys in this course. You all began the course at different starting points. Your various backgrounds and personal and professional accumulations of experience differ widely. Because of that, some of you were/are more cognitively ready than others to accommodate, assimilate, and ultimately transform the information being presented. As well, your varying philosophies, world views, and ethics are influencing your availability to relate to and connect with that information. On top of that, your varying personal and professional circumstances naturally result in some of you having greater access to learning (more time to internalize the information and/or more opportunity to apply the information {learn further by doing}) than others. Again, these are the reasons why grading is a discriminatory practice. And finally, your willingness to comply (i.e., the amount of effort you're willing to put into internalizing and applying the course information) differs for each of you as well.

If we are not ready or able to accept that grading is discriminatory then let's look at grading from another angle and ask ourselves these questions. What *constructive* purpose would it serve me to "correct" the tasks you just completed, tally your individual scores, and then insert them into a comparative cut-score-grading-scale and grade you against each other?

First, what purpose does it serve to convert your score into a grade, period? Asked another way, what purpose does is serve to grade your score (which is essentially all we're doing when we convert scores into grades)?

And second, **what would the grade tell you and me about your individual learning (and you as a learner) that your score doesn't already tell us?** For that matter, what does the score tell us that the completed tasks themselves (i.e., your classroom formative assessment portfolio) don't already tell us?

Is Your School's Report Card Truly Standards-based?

One of the requirements in our graduate program for teachers is a course on transforming grading practices. In this course teachers take a hard look at whether grades concocted through averaging, weighting, composite grading, giving zeros, and using random grading curves are valid, reliable, and fair. They explore diverse theories, all of which ultimately reveal that learning is not a summative but rather a formative, constructive process. And when they deduce from those theories how unfair it is to give students from disparate backgrounds an equal amount of time to progress in the standards and then, when that time is up, comparatively grade (rank and label) them based on their relative proficiencies most are greatly disturbed over what for them is now a moral dilemma. They recognize grading is flawed, fallacious, and discriminatory but they are mandated to grade their students.

When we go from there to exploring standards-based scoring as an alternative to grading the general reaction among the teachers is, "This makes total sense. This is what I want to be doing, not grading."

With standards-based scoring the student receives two scores ... a progress score and a grade level score. But to understand how that works we need to back up.

Standards-based scoring and reporting is part of a larger standards-based formative instruction and assessment process. With this process there is a core set of power standards embedded in everything that's taught. Power standards are the standards that truly have enduring value beyond school, value across multiple disciplines, and ensure student readiness for the next level of learning (Ainsworth, 2004). For every power standard there is a progress rubric. Standards-based formative assessment is a daily part of instruction and the resulting student work is kept in the student's classroom formative assessment portfolio. Periodically throughout the marking period the student's latest body of work is measured up against the standards-based progress rubrics, and the rubrics are dated accordingly. Then at reporting time the student receive two scores for each power standard.

The progress score is the number of criteria per standard in which the student is demonstrating sustained growth at the time of reporting. For example, let's say Power Standard Z has five criteria. If the student's latest body of work shows that she has grown or is at least sustaining her competency in three of those five criteria since the last time her growth was marked on the rubric her progress score for that standard would be 3/5 or 60%.

The grade level score is the number of criteria in which the student has reached the third column on the progress rubric, commonly considered the "At Standard Grade Level" column. With the student above, if at reporting time her work places her in the third benchmark box for two of the five criteria her grade level score would be 2/5 or 40%. She is at grade level in two of the standard's five criteria.

These two **scores** are what get reported on a standards-based report card.

At this point in the course we discuss scores vs. grades. Scores, like those above, are simply reported as is. They are not inserted into a comparative cut-score grading scale (i.e., categorized as "Beyond, At, or Below Standard") and converted into grades at the conclusion of a set time frame such as a marking period. When that is done students end up being ranked against a common timed finish line despite not all being on the same starting line (schematically) at the beginning of the marking period. To do that would be discriminatory.

"This makes so much sense. But we still have to give grades. We aren't allowed to just give scores."

And so we look at how teachers can incorporate this formative process as much as possible given the constraints of their summative "standards-based" report cards.

For teachers who have to give just an ABCDF, the conversion is simple. If there are ten power standards, some of those standards will have five criteria, some will have four, others six, and so on. If a grade has to be given that means there has to be a cut-score grading scale involved. So the teachers simply determine a common cut-score scale for all standards with four criteria, one for all standards with five criteria, etc. For example, a cut-score scale for power standards with five criteria might be 5-4=A, 3=B, 2=C, 1=D, 0=F. So in the case of our student above her progress score of 3/5 would result in a progress *grade* of B, and her grade level score of 2/5 would equate to a grade level *grade* of C.

These are grades, and they're discriminatory. But the compromise for now is that these grades are based on a student's *growth* in the standards, not her comparative attainment of them.

At this point in the course teachers who have to use report cards with a grading scale of 4=Beyond Standard, 3=At Standard, 2= Below Standard, 1=Introductory become quite agitated. They are frustrated at discovering that their "standards-based" report card doesn't accommodate standards-based *progress* scoring. For example, on their report card the progress score of 3/5 for the student above would give her a progress *grade* of 3=At Standard. But what if her progress was she reached the first column on the rubric for her very first time? That's cause for celebration but being in the first column on the rubric doesn't qualify as At Standard Grade Level. *When these teachers realize that their so-called "standards-based" report cards don't honor every child's progress they feel even more defeated.*

If they could simply change their report card's cut-score grading scale to 4=*Showing growth in all of the standard's criteria, 3=Showing growth in most of the standard's criteria (most meaning half or more), 2= Showing growth in some of standard's criteria (some meaning less than half), 1= Not showing growth in any of the standard's criteria at this time* the problem would be solved. Their report card would align with the formative nature of learning and they would have a true standards-based report card.

But it's the rare district that has the courage to say no to the use of discriminatory grading scales such as Above Standard – At Standard – Below Standard.

These "standards-based" report cards are no different than any other traditional report card. A true standards-based report card aligns with what cognitive science has revealed about learning. Learning is a formative process and a learner's schema is never static but constantly evolving. Consequently, any grade we give is instantly obsolete. Here's a simple example of this. When we give a student a test, grade it, put written feedback on it, and give it back to the student to review, as he interacts with that feedback his cognition of the material on the test changes. *And just like that the grade is no longer relevant.*

And with regard to the standards, there is no finality with them either. The more we engage our students deeper and wider in the standards the more their competency in those standards will grow. Unlike traditional knowledge acquisition curricula there is no "they either got it or they didn't" summation point with standards-based curricula.

Grading has no place in standards-based formative instruction and assessment and reporting. One very simple way to know whether your report card is truly standards-based is to observe classroom instruction. If students are still being graded on their acquisition of unit-specific content, their homework and classwork are still being graded, and/or the practices of averaging, weighting, composite grading, giving zeros, and arbitrary use of cut-score grading scales are still in use the report card accompanying those practices can't possibly be a true standards-based report card.

Standards-Based Report Cards

Having the standards listed on the report card, as opposed to subject areas (e.g., Math, Science, etc.) does not necessarily mean it's a standards-based report card. Using a 4-3-2-1 grading system rather than the traditional ABCDF system doesn't mean it's standards-based either.

It's not the report card itself that makes it a standards-based report card it's whether true standards-based formative instruction and assessment is occurring in every classroom that makes it standards-based.

And with standards-based formative instruction and assessment the students' report grades are no longer based on the students' recall/retention (or how many they got right vs. wrong) of subject area content, their ability to perform lesson-specific skills, or their ability to meet lesson-specific expectations. Instead, their "grades" (preferably scores) are based on their growth in the actual criteria of the actual academic standards they're working on.

If the report card still lists subject areas, like Social Studies, as long as the students' grades are no longer an average of the grades they got on their civics, westward expansion, and Latin America unit tests and the various tasks they completed during those units but rather on the number of power standards (being taught within the "Social Studies" curriculum) the students are showing sustained growth in at the time of reporting, it would still be a standards-based report card. But why continue to list subject areas rather than the standards?

Grading Aha #2 Relative to Constructive Learning

If we correct a student's work, score it (e.g., +43/50), put instructive, narrative feedback on it to help the student further learn the topic of that work (all of which we are responsible for doing), grade it, and then return it to the student as feedback, the instant the student interacts with that feedback her schema changes ... and consequently the grade she received is instantly obsolete. So if we truly are using student work formatively, then what are we doing with those obsolete grades, and what purpose (a purpose the score itself can't serve) is it serving to even give those grades in the first place?

Grading Aha #2 Stated Differently

We grade a student's test, give it back to him, and through either written or verbal feedback we talk with him about where he was "right," where he was "wrong," and why. As he interacts with that feedback his cognition of the content of the test is changing. The grade he received at this point is no longer relevant. It is not an accurate measurement anymore of where his knowledge construct now is.

But despite this, the grade typically stands and remains as part of his record. But of what value is that grade if it's already obsolete? And then to compound the issue, that grade is then usually averaged in with all the previous grades he received, which are also obsolete, and subsequent grades he will be receiving (which in no time will also become obsolete). So what value is his grade average (final grade) and what does that final grade/average actually reflect?

"You Can Still Grade Formative Assessments, Can't You?"

If a teacher does an assessment initially intended to be used formatively, and then decides to grade it, technically and theoretically that "assessment" has now become a summative evaluation.

And what happens with summative evaluations (graded stuff)? They get incorporated into the student's overall grade via averaging and weighting, perhaps along with some zeros, and therefore can never be an accurate measure of student learning. Why? Because we know the mathematical process of averaging can't possibly produce a quantitative measure that represents the student's actual knowledge construct (schema development/state of learning) at the time of grading and reporting ... which is what grades, report cards, and progress reports are supposed to do. An average represents some earlier state of the student's learning because it incorporates grades the student received during his earlier stages of learning the material. And that's just the flaw of averaging! The flaws of weighting and giving zeros relative to accurately quantifying a student's present state of knowledge construction are even more obvious.

Hopefully, the teacher asking this question was really asking, "Formative assessments can still be *scored*, right?" Absolutely! If there were ten possible answers for the activity and the student got eight out of the ten, there is nothing wrong with letting the student know that *this* time she got a score of 8/10 or 80%, and then discuss with her what strategy she might try to get a nine or ten out of ten next time. Remember, grading and scoring are nowhere close to being a one in the same practice.

So back to grading formative assessment ... The teacher most likely will still use the assessment "sort of formatively" (i.e., let the results of that "assessment" drive her subsequent planning and instruction) but by grading it, which the grade will no doubt get incorporated into some kind of averaging and weighting scheme, the teacher will be using it summatively. When you look at the true definitions of "formative" and "summative," as well as assessment and evaluation, you will see that formative and summative are antithetical. Given that, how can a single "assessment" be both? Grading an assessment defeats its purpose. By all means score them. However, as James Popham states in his recent book, *Transformative Assessment* (2008), "Keep grades out of it."

Three Large-Scale Problematic Practices around Grading

The first is grading student work rather than simply scoring it. What purpose does converting scores into grades serve? Why bother grading the student's score, which is all we are really doing when we convert a score into a grade? Does converting a score into a grade improve student learning?

The second problematic practice is unit-based teaching and grading versus standards-based instruction and assessment. With unit-based teaching a specific amount of time is allocated to covering some particular content, and then when the unit is done we give the student a final grade and move on to the next unit. All aspects of what was just described fly in the face of what cognitive science and constructivism say about how true learning occurs. There is no finality with continually making connections and building our knowledge constructs.

Standards-based formative instruction and assessment accompanied with progress scoring is a process that aligns with what we know about learning and how learning occurs because it's a process that's seamless and for which there is not finality.

And the third problematic practice is assigning grades within one-size-fits-all time frames (e.g., length of a unit, making period, school year). No matter how much individualized differentiated instruction, assessment, and evaluation (if required) we do, whether comparatively norm-referenced or individually criterion-referenced, all of our students still get graded at the same END time (end of unit, end of marking period). But we know that not everyone can or does learn at the same rate because of how varied their knowledge constructs are when they all start out together at the same START time (beginning of unit, beginning of marking period).

One-size-fits-all grading time frames is the overriding, underlying, mostly unrecognized, insidious norm against which we are all, mostly unwittingly, comparatively norm-referencing our students and consequently discriminating against most of them.

Alternatives to Traditional Grading: Some Small Steps to Try

There are several alternatives to traditional grading, a practice we now understand to be inherently discriminatory. One is to simply stop at the scoring stage and not take that next step of converting the students' scores into grades. In other words, just report the score, don't insert the score into a cut-score grading scale. If you work in a system in which you have to give a grade, although the following alternatives will not erase the discrimination factor, they will address other validity issues surrounding grading.

One of those alternatives is to use differentiated cut-score grading scales rather than one-size-fits-all scales. To be fair a cut-score scale should at least be proportional to the number of criteria being scored and graded. For example, if would not be fair, valid, reliable, or meaningful to use the same cut-score scale for tasks with 100 items and for tasks with 20 items.

A second alternative is to tally up the student's total points for the marking period and then place that score in a cut-score grading scale appropriate to the grand total of potential points. You'll still be grading but at least you won't be doing any averaging.

Doing away with giving zeros is a third alternative. In a 90-100=A, 80-89=B, etc. scale a zero has a disproportionate and unfair effect on a student's overall average because of the 49 point increment between 49 and 0 versus the ten point increments from the A down to the F. If you are doing alternative two (above) giving zeros would not be unfair.

Conducting skill-specific grading as opposed to composite grading is an important fourth alternative to consider. Composite grading is the practice of combining grades that students receive in a range of different skills (e.g., test scores, homework completion, participation, neatness, etc.) and then averaging them all together into one summative grade. The problems with composite grading are many, two of the more overt problems being 1) the practice typically involves averaging and weighting (weighting inherently favors some learning styles over others) and 2) the overall grade does not inform us as to exactly what the student knows and is able to do, nor does it identify the skills in which the student is strong and not so strong.

A fifth alternative is to only grade "final" efforts rather than early efforts. "Final" is in quotation marks for two reasons. First, there is no finality in knowledge construction. Second, by final we don't mean literally the last activity through which the student is given the opportunity to demonstrate their proficiency. No single assessment can ever be a valid and reliable assessment of a student's overall proficiency. By not grading early efforts you would be acknowledging the fact that learning is a process, knowledge undergoes construction, and that process takes time. What purpose would it serve the student to grade her learning in its infancy? By not grading early efforts you would also not be factoring in those "learning in its infancy" grades when you go to total or average their final grades. If you did you would effectively punish the student for not having a more advanced level of knowledge right from the start.

And last, but definitely not least, grading student *progress* as opposed to grading their level of attainment would be taking a giant step away from discriminatory grading practices. Again, because grading would still be occurring with this alternative, so would discrimination. But criterion-referenced, progress-based grading is far less discriminatory than norm-referenced, attainment-based grading.

Progress

Constructivist learning theory reveals that a) learning is a formative process, and b) learning is a continual work-in-progress (it's never static and there's no finality to it). If learning is formative then it makes sense that the way in which we monitor our students' learning should be formative as well. In other words, we should be relying solely on formative assessment, not summative evaluation. And if learning is a continual work-in-progress then it also makes sense we should monitor and report our students' *progress*. Said differently, we should be relying on progress rubrics (see Section Five) not attainment-oriented rubrics and their accompanying cut-score grading scales (i.e., 4-3-2-1 or Above Standard-At Standard-Below Standard.

Progress, Take Two

Progress is an organic component of constructivist learning, formative assessment, and standards-based instruction. Learning is the act of constructing knowledge. Constructing knowledge is a (building) process. Any process automatically entails progress.

The standards are lifelong learning skills and concepts that are inherently about knowledge construction, not simply information retention. And with construction of knowledge there is no finality and therefore there is no finality with standards. Striving to become more and more proficient in a standard is a process and as with any process, for it to unfold there automatically has to be sustained progress. Because there is no finality, attainment can only ever be relative, and true "attainment" is impossible. "Attaining the Standard," "Achieving the Standard," "Meeting the Standard," and being "At Standard" are nothing more than some commonly agreed-upon level of proficiency someone deemed "good enough." They are arbitrary finish lines drawn somewhere amidst lifelong learning.

Formative assessment is the process of continually monitoring and measuring learning as it emerges and develops ("forms"), while at the same time continually gathering feedback and responding to that feedback in a way that shapes ("forms") both the learner's subsequent learning and the teacher's subsequent instruction. It is a never ending cycle in which teaching and learning both shape and are shaped by one another. Formative assessment, itself, is a process ... a process of monitoring the student's knowledge construction (also a process) as her learning *progresses*.

Given how organic progress is to teaching and learning doesn't it make sense that student **progress** be our primary focus when it comes to instruction, assessment, evaluation, and reporting of student learning?

Progress, Progress, Progress

Learning is a constructivist, formative process. Our backgrounds, which are shaped by what we experience, shape our ever-expanding schemas (cognitive frameworks) and ever-evolving gestalts (world views), which in turn shape how we interact with subsequent experiences, which in turn shape our ever-expanding knowledge constructs (schemas), which in turn shapes our ever-evolving mental frameworks (gestalts) ... did anyone else suddenly just find themselves humming, "And the wheels on the bus ..."?

Teaching and learning is a formative process, too. Our teaching shapes our students' learning, which in turn shapes our learning, in turn shaping our teaching, which in turn further shapes our students' learning, etc., etc., etc.

It makes sense that (formative) assessment and instruction go hand in hand. And if there is no finality to learning and learning is ever-evolving, never static, then it also makes sense that the only thing we can legitimately monitor and report on is our students' **progress** (growth)... hence the formative assessment accompanied by progress rubrics we're exploring in this course (now this book, Section Five).

~ V ~

A PROGRESSIVE ALTERNATIVE

A Proposition

Given that teaching and learning are intrinsically formative, so too should be the way in which we monitor, measure, and report student learning. We should be monitoring student learning by way of formative assessment rather than summative evaluation, which in turn means focusing on student *progress* rather than attainment, and using criterion-referenced measurements rather than norm-referenced measurements ... all of which means we should be ultimately measuring and reporting student learning using scores rather than grades.

Progress, Take Three

Progressive thought supports progress over attainment

According to systems theory everything is in a perpetual state of evolution. Thus, nothing ever reaches a point of *true* finality. Consequently, levels of "attainment" are merely someone's arbitrary finish lines prematurely drawn somewhere in mid-progress.

According to constructivism knowledge and understanding are in a perpetual state of evolution, continually being shaped and re-shaped.

According to the theory of phenomenology reality is fluid, sub-jective, and context dependent. Truth is relative to culture. In short, everything is relative and nothing is fixed.

Progressive thought supports assessment over evaluation

Assessment is an inherent part of systems dynamics and critical to sustainability. It is a natural, cyclical, internal feedback process that stimulates continual self-reorganization and self-renewal. As-sessment stimulates continual growth and transformation of the system's parts, thereby promoting sustainability of the system as a whole.

In contrast, evaluation-minded instruction is linear (an input-output approach striving toward an illusory end point) and eval-uation, itself, is an unnatural, externally imposed attempt to simplistically and quantitatively capture, condense, define, fix, and categorize how much learning has taken place. But learning is a complex process that is ever-expanding, interpretive, and fluid ... a process for which there is no finality.

Proposition

Based on our systems understanding that:

- learning is in a perpetual state of construction
- learning curves are influenced by a complex of identifiable and unidentifiable variables
- learning curves vary/can vary widely from one individual to the next
- true attainment is unattainable
- everything is open to interpretation
- there are serious flaws inherent in evaluation

Monitoring and measuring (i.e., assessing) students' individual **progress** rather than comparatively evaluating (grading) them based on "attainment" is the only fair, valid, and ecologically sound thing we can and should be doing with our students.

The Disconnect with Grading

Inherent in both constructivist learning and academic standards is infinite growth. And growth automatically entails *progress*. There is no finality with either learning or potential growth in the standards.

Constructivist learning and academic standards are natural partners with formative assessment. Formative assessment is the process of monitoring and responding to growth (progress), and progress (growth) is a natural part of any formative process.

Inherent in grading, however, is finality, not continuous growth. Grades are final, fixed values representing one's level of attainment. Progress is not fixed. It's potentially infinite.

If there is no finality in learning, if construction of knowledge is a potentially infinite process, and if the complex of external factors outside of our control that shape our knowledge constructs (schemas) naturally and widely vary from one individual to the next, then doesn't it make sense that the only ethical and responsible way to account for student learning is to measure and report their personal **progress** (growth) rather than their comparative attainment?

There is a way to do this that is valid, reliable and informative, maintains rigor, empowers students, holds students accountable, provides external motivation for those students who need it, and does not involve the discriminatory practice of grading. That approach is standards-based, formative instruction and assessment and criterion-referenced, progress-based scoring and reporting.

Standards- and Assessment-Based Scoring

The process of standards- and assessment-based scoring involves the use of generalized-standard *progress* rubrics (assessment tools). Below are some of the many benefits that collaboratively developed progress rubrics provide:

- They list the criteria which comprise and define the actual standards students are accountable for growing in.
- They list the criteria that we will use to guide our planning and drive our instruction and assessment (i.e., keep us focused and purposeful).
- They list the benchmarks against which we can actually measure student performance and thereby actually know whether a student is progressing in the criteria of those standards.
- They list criteria that explicitly define for the students what's important and benchmarks that explicitly describe what is being expected of them.
- They serve as tools for providing feedback and formally monitoring, recording, documenting, and reporting student progress.
- They reinforce ("force") the provision of multiple opportunities (formative assessments) for students to engage in the standards.
- They provide an effective and efficient way to enhance inclusive assessment for these tools can be used by multiple stakeholders.
- They enable consistent, valid, reliable, and equitable assessment of student progress.
- They provide an effective and efficient mechanism through which to implement a K-12 portfolio system/process.
- They provide the mechanism we need to efficiently, validly, reliably, fairly, and objectively convert assessment data into grades for institutions still requiring that grades be given.

This process involves no averaging, no weighting, no composite grading, no zeros, and is not subject to unfair cut-score grading scales. It allows for simultaneous assessment (and evaluation if necessary) of student proficiency in delineated criteria of each standard as well as the standards as wholes. It involves measuring student progress rather than attainment. And, it results in scores (grades if necessary) that genuinely reflect student progress in the actual standards rather than achievement of arbitrary task-specific, teacher-specific, and content-specific expectations.

Generalized-Standard Progress Rubrics

Some of the major benefits of generalized-standard progress rubrics include:

The criteria listed down the left hand side of each rubric are the criteria that comprise the standard. The criteria are the standard and vice versa. These rubrics keep us focused on both the standards' parts as well as the standards as wholes.

1. They keep us focused on the ultimate aspects of proficiency in the knowledge and skills we want our students to know and be able to do by the time they leave school ... those aspects of proficiency being independence, accuracy, relevance, amount, and span.
2. They hold us accountable for ensuring that students are being provided multiple opportunities in the standards over time and across contexts, and they enable us to monitor and measure student progress/growth.
3. They serve as tools that enable us to derive valid, reliable, and fair scores (and grades if necessary) that are truly standards-based scores (grades).
4. They serve as tools that enable us to do pure criterion-referenced, progress-based scoring and reporting.

Generalized-Standard Progress Rubrics:
Attributes Continued

Some of their many attributes include:

• align with constructivist learning theory and what we know about how learning occurs

- naturally promote a greater emphasis on knowledge construction over information retention
- help ensure that the standards are the primary focus in the classroom
- do not involve use of cut-score grading scales which are a) discriminatory, and b)whose proficiency labels (e.g., Beyond Standard – At Standard, etc.) tend to be equated with traditional grades
- are criterion-referenced not norm-referenced
- are progress-based not attainment-based
- inherently account for student effort and no subjective or separate effort grades need to be given
- work independently of the number of opportunities students are afforded by their respective teachers, thereby avoiding equity and fairness issues
- naturally promote and enforce standards-based instruction and assessment because in order for them to work the teacher has to be providing students multiple opportunities in each standard over time and across contexts
- hold both the teacher and student accountable which helps naturally promote a formative teaching and learning cycle
- naturally promote both formative and differentiated instruction and assessment
- naturally promote greater student ownership
- provide a framework for a credible, informative, and easy to maintain PK-12 student portfolio system
- do not involve grading students and therefore do not involve averaging, weighting, composite grading, or giving zeros
- reinforce for students the notion of lifelong learning and that there's no finality to learning
- are more valid than current, conventional means of grading and reporting student learning

An Example of a Generalized-Standard Progress Rubric

Below is a sample of a standards-based progress rubric for a math standard for mathematical computation and applying mathematical strategies.

Standard: Mathematical Computation and Strategy Application

Student's Name: _____

Independently and accurately computes*	Occasionally	Regularly	Frequently	Always (f)
	In at least one context	In a few different contexts	In several different contexts	In many different contexts (s)
Independently and relevantly applies strategies*	Occasionally	Regularly	Frequently	Always (f)
	In a few different contexts	In several different contexts	In many different contexts	In every context experienced (s)
.	One or two strategies	A few strategies	Several strategies	Many strategies (a)

*See student's classroom formative assessment portfolio for evidence
Aspects of Proficiency being measured: independence, accuracy, relevance, frequency (f), span(s), and amount (a)
Additional Comments/Observations:

Creating Standards-Based Progress Rubrics

What follows is the process for developing any standards-based progress rubric. We'll look specifically at the steps taken to create the sample rubric above. The two criteria of this standard are computation and applying strategies. They are listed down the left hand side of the rubric and notice the two criteria are generalized, not specific to any particular task. There are six common aspects of proficiency for which students and student work are commonly measured. Each needs to be considered as to whether they apply to each standard for which a progress rubric is being created.

The first aspect of proficiency is *independence* ... can the child express the knowledge he's acquiring or perform the skill he's learning on his own without needing help, support, or prompting? In other words, has he truly internalized the knowledge or skill? Given that the standards are what we want our students to know and be able to do by the time they leave high school, independence should be measured no matter which standard or criterion is being addressed.

For each of the standards' criteria some, and in some cases perhaps all, of the remaining five aspects of proficiency that follow will also apply and therefore be important to measure.

Accuracy ... does the child perform the skill accurately? For example, it does matter how accurately a child can compute. Therefore, "accuracy" applies to our first criterion.

Relevance ... is what the child has done relevant to the task or topic at hand? For example, it matters that the child applies strategies in a relevant manner. So in this case, "relevantly" does apply to our second criterion.

Because the above three aspects of proficiency are relatively definitive (i.e., the child is either doing it independently or she's not, it's either accurate or it isn't, and it's either relevant or it isn't) they can be incorporated directly into the wording of the criterion itself and do not need to be broken out into an escalating continuum of benchmarks. At this point our progress rubric looks like this:

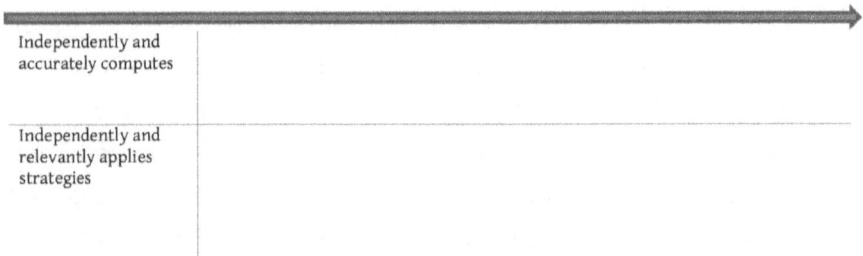

Independently and accurately computes	
Independently and relevantly applies strategies	

The remaining three aspects of proficiency are frequency, amount, and span.

Frequency ... how often is the child able to demonstrate the skill? For example, it matters that the child can perform a basic math skill time and time again.

Amount ... how many is the child able to perform? In the case of spelling, for example, we care about how many words the child is able to spell correctly.

Span ... is the child able to demonstrate the skill across different contexts or in different situations? For example, does the child demonstrate teamwork skills no matter who she works with, and on no matter what project she is working? A second example is does the child apply her scientific method skills (observation, questioning, hypothesizing, etc.) in contexts other than science?

Unlike the first three, these three aspects of proficiency are not definitive. There are degrees of competency within which a child's performance can fall. Consequently, these aspects of proficiency do need to be broken out into a continuum that reflects growth. For example, the continuum for frequency might be occasionally-regularly-frequently-always

Both frequency and span apply to "accurately computes." It matters how often a child can compute accurately and it matters that he can do it in different contexts. Our second criterion is "relevantly applies strategies" and in this case frequency, span, and amount all apply.

After the aspects of proficiency have been decided on for each criterion, the performance continua for "frequency," "amount," and "span" have to be determined. In this case it was decided the continuum for "frequency" would be occasionally-regularly-frequently-always. Once each row of benchmark boxes is completed for each criterion and its corresponding aspects of proficiency, two steps remain. List the aspects of proficiency being assessed and provide a space for the assessor to be able to write comments and observations she may have regarding the student's progress (see completed rubric above).

Progress Rubric Benchmarks

"Instead of terms like few, several, many and occasionally, regularly, frequently why don't we just use actual numbers?"

There are two key reasons why actual numbers generally do not work on formative progress rubrics. First, keep in mind that these progress rubrics are for our power standards. That means they are common rubrics being used by multiple teachers across classrooms and subject areas. Not every teacher teaching and assessing students in those power standards will have equal time and access to students. Some teachers will be able to provide their students many opportunities to grow in a particular standard, while others will only be able to provide their students a few opportunities.

Second, keeping in mind the nature of formative instruction and assessment, we can't possibly know ahead of time what actual number will be achievable by the end of a marking period or the school year.

Let's look further at this issue of using actual numbers by looking specifically at "frequency." The following discussion also applies to "span."

Frequency is the number of times the student demonstrated the skill out of the total number of opportunities she was given. If we were to put a continuum of actual numbers for our benchmarks, for example 1-3 times-4-6 times-7-9 times-10-12 times, one or both of the following are very likely to happen and render our rubric useless. First, our ongoing formative assessments of our students might reveal that the students continue to need a lot more teaching, modeling, and practice of the skill than we thought. By the time we're able to start assessing whether they can independently demonstrate the skill they might not have sufficient time/opportunities to get up to 7-9 times (which, in this example is the "At Standard" or "3" expectation).

Second, some teachers might be able to give their students plenty of opportunities to get up to 7-9 times but for a variety of legitimate reasons other teachers might not. The latter teacher's students will never get the chance to reach "At Standard (at grade level)" which a) would not be fair, and b) raises the question whether an actual number can be valid or is simply arbitrary and subjective ... which is especially concerning when it comes to "at grade level" numbers that are assigned.

With terms such as occasionally, regularly, and frequently regardless of the number of opportunities teachers are able to give their students these measures will still apply. If students in one classroom only get five opportunities within a marking period, according to our collaboratively determined definitions of these three terms if a student independently demonstrates the skill five times that qualifies as "always," four times would be "frequently," three times is "regularly," one or two times is "occasionally," and zero times is not yet on the rubric.

In the classroom next door where students might have had fifteen opportunities during the marking period fifteen is "always," twelve to fourteen is "frequently," eight to eleven is "regularly," one to seven is "occasionally," and zero is not yet on the rubric.

In short, every student has an equal opportunity to get to the commonly agreed upon "at grade level ("At Standard" or"3") benchmark with these "qualitative" quantitative benchmarks. And of course the students' actual numbers (e.g., 2/5 or 11/15) can always be listed in the "Additional Comments/Observations" section at the bottom of the rubric if that information is meaningful.

Depending on the specific criterion being measured one possible exception to using "occasionally," "regularly," and "frequently" might be to use percentage of time instead ... for example, 1-32% of the time, 33-65% of the time, etc. If percentages are used it is critical that the words "of the time" are included in the benchmark so stakeholders don't mistake these percentages as grades. There is an extra computation step with this approach which will require more of a teacher's time, and some stakeholders will balk at the wide range within percentage benchmarks. For example, there's a significant difference between performing the skill 66% of the time versus 99% of the time.

And finally, the third aspect of proficiency that sometimes applies to certain criteria and is included as benchmarks is "amount."

Amount is different than frequency. Amount is the number of something the student knows or uses or can do, not the number of times she shows she can do it. With amount, actual numbers can work but only in cases where there are a fixed number of possibilities and the student has been taught all of them. For example, if we're assessing the students' competency at using problem solving strategies and there are ten known strategies and all of them have been taught, then our four point continuum of benchmarks might be 1-3, 4-6, 7-9, and 10. In this example students being able to use 7-9 strategies by the end of the school year will be at our agreed upon "at grade level" benchmark.

An Example of How Progress Rubrics Work

August 28 (First day of the school year)

Give the students copies of the power standard progress rubrics you and they will be using (working from and toward) throughout the year. Review the standards, criteria, benchmarks, and the six aspects of proficiency with your students. It is critically important teachers discuss the definitions for "independently," "relevantly," and "accurately" at the start of each school year when the students receive their standards-based progress rubrics. Terms being used as benchmarks for "frequency," "amount," and "span" will also need to be defined up front. For example, definitions for terms used for the "frequency" continuum in our sample above might be: occasionally = from time to time; now and then; once in a while; regularly = usually; generally; most of the time; more times than not; frequently = almost always; just short of always; not quite every time.

Starting tomorrow (August 29) begin engaging your students in enabling activities purposefully designed to draw out the students' ability in the criteria of your year-long standards (power standards).

September 15

You are now a half a month or so into the school year and it is time to start doing baseline assessments of your students. For example, let's say by September 15 the student has had five opportunities (three performances and two tasks) to engage in, and thereby be assessed in, Standard X. Those six enabling activities (student work that serves as evidence of proficiency) are in the student's classroom formative assessment portfolio. Based on that collective data as a whole mark the student on their progress rubric and date each benchmark box in which the student has landed at this time.

October 10

Since the first rubric was filled out back on September 15 the student has had eight more opportunities (four performances, two tasks, one product, and she completed one self-assessment rubric) to engage in Standard X. Those eight pieces of evidence are now also in the student's formative assessment portfolio. Based on this latest round of collective data, mark the student on their progress rubric and date each mark accordingly.

November 13

Since the second rubric was completed back on October 10 the student has had five more opportunities (three performances, one task, and one product) to engage in the criteria of Standard X. Those pieces of student work are in the student's portfolio. Based on this latest round of collective data again mark the student on the rubric and date accordingly.

Are We Back to Averaging?

"When we look at a body of work and then measure it up against the frequency benchmarks on the progress rubric isn't that still averaging?"

This is a great question and, knowing what we know about averaging, a concern definitely worth addressing. So let's take a look.

Let's say from the start of the school year up to September 21 we are able to engage our students in six power standard-based formative instruction and assessment activities. Consequently, we have

six pieces of evidence of learning in our students' classroom formative assessment portfolios. And after collecting the sixth piece we
decide to pause and check in on how well the student is progressing
in these six standards.

We look at all six pieces of dated student work as a whole, as
one entity, and we measure that body of evidence up against the
frequency benchmarks which are, from left to right, "occasionally,"
"regularly," "frequently," and "always." We see that the student
has demonstrated the skill two out of the six times (2/6) she worked
on it. Based on collaboratively agreed upon definitions for the frequency benchmarks two out of six times qualifies as "occasionally."
So in the "occasionally" box we write the date 9/21. This lets stakeholders know that as of September 21 the student is able to demonstrate the skill on an occasional basis. The two out of six (2/6) is not
an average, it's simply a total score.

*"But what if, when looking at her six pieces of work, we see that she
was unable to demonstrate the skill her first two attempts but then demonstrated it four straight times after that. For those last four pieces she
demonstrated the skill "always," and for the first two she demonstrated it
"never." Four times out of six qualifies as "regularly" but at this time she's
doing it every time so isn't "regularly" essentially an average and not a true
reflection of her actual proficiency at the time of reporting?"*

Again, this is an excellent question and on the surface the answer appears to be yes. But the answer is actually no. No actual average was computed, it is simply her total that is being incorporated
into the rubric.

Now, unlike with averaging, a few weeks later when we measure
the student's latest round (since 9/21) of work up against the
benchmarks the previous "regularly" becomes extinct. If we were
averaging, that "regularly" would remain with the student forever
because it would continue to be part of her overall average. It would
also prevent her from ever being able to achieve a rate of "always."
But because with progress rubrics we only measure the student's
newest round of work - work done since the last time her growth

was marked on the rubric – that "regularly" does not factor in any-where.

So in this example where the student demonstrated the skill four straight times prior to September 21 but only got a "regularly," if she has truly internalized the skill and from September 21 to let's say October 15, the next time we mark her on the rubric, demon-strated the skill every chance she had she will land in the "always" box, something she could never do if we continued to factor in her initial "regularly."

This example also addresses two other things related to progress rubrics. First, just because a student demonstrates a skill X number of times in a row doesn't necessarily mean she's internalized the skill. Can she continually do it time and time again? And if she does not engage in that skill for a while and then later does, can she still do it after being away from it for a while?

And second, in a case like this where the student was unable to demonstrate the skill her first two tries but then did four straight times after that the teacher would definitely want to write that in the "Additional Comments/Observations" section on the rubric to put more context to the "regularly" the student was credited for.

When Do I Mark the Students on Our Progress Rubrics?

- You do not have to mark every student in your classroom at the same time on these power standard progress rubrics. Stagger and spread them out over time. Remember, these are your power standards. You will be engaging your students in these standards over time and across contexts, all year long.
- For the same reason you do not have to mark the students on every one of your power standard progress rubrics at the same time. Mark them when you've gathered sufficient evi-dence (student work) per power standard.
- You do not mark a student on the rubric after each enabling activity, as is done with traditional activity-specific rubrics

and checklists. For one, the benchmarks and six aspects of proficiency (e.g., "in several different contexts" and "frequently") on a *progress* rubric won't allow you to. Secondly, these are *progress* rubrics on which the students' progress over time is being measured. The idea is to wait until the student has done a number of enabling activities (products, performances, tasks) and you've been able to make a number of anecdotal observations before you and your students sit down, look at their work cumulatively, and then mark them on their rubrics.

• You do not have to mark the students in every criterion listed down the left hand side of the rubric every time you check in and complete a rubric on them. Some criteria might be getting addressed more and sooner than others, and some criteria and their corresponding benchmarks of growth will require less evidence to begin marking than others. For those criteria that require more time and evidence, wait until adequate time and evidence have accumulated.

Reminders

1. Internalize the criteria of your power standards and continually work from and toward your power standard progress rubrics. As opposed to your content and prior units of study you created, the criteria of these standards are now your new lens/filter.
2. Remember, you do not have to be doing every criterion all the time and with every activity that you do with your students.
3. You will be working on these standards all year long. You have all year and lots of time and chances to teach and assess your students in the criteria of these power standards.
4. You do not have to "rubricize" every activity or every student every day.
5. Stagger when, how often, and who you assess.

6. Stagger when, how often, and who you "rubricize."
7. Develop enabling activities purposefully designed to *draw out* student performance of the criteria in which you are trying to assess your students.
8. Do not stretch or contrive activities in an attempt to "cover" particular criteria. You won't get the data you're trying to get, the students will see right through your attempt, and all you'll end up doing is just that ... covering it rather than enabling them to learn and grow in it.

Measuring and Scoring Student Progress

The student's standards-based progress score is simply the number of the standard's criteria out of the standard's total number of criteria in which the student has demonstrated growth (progress or sustained competency) since the last time the student was scored on the rubric for that particular standard. For example, if the standard has five criteria and the student's latest round of collective work (produced from the multiple opportunities provided over time and across contexts for the student to work on the criteria of that standard) since the last time the student was scored on the rubric shows evidence the student has grown in four of those five criteria, the student's standards-based progress score for that standard would be 4 out of 5 or 4/5 or 80% ... period.

Important things to recognize regarding standard-based progress scoring include:

- It relies on the use of generalized-standard progress rubrics as opposed to task/activity-specific rubrics or checklists (tools used to drive lesson-specific instruction and provide students with lesson-specific feedback)
- It is pure criterion-referencing versus norm referencing (i.e., assessing student proficiency in specific criteria versus comparatively grading them against some norm)
- It promotes differentiated instruction

- It eliminates the use of cut-score grading scales, averaging, weighting, composite grading, and giving zeros ... all practices with fairness, equity, reliability, and validity problems
- It does not discriminate against students
- It does not allow for any student to "coast." Every student is held accountable for showing continued growth no matter where he/she is on the rubric
- It is credible, defensible, and more objective than traditional grading
- It empowers students to have greater control over their own learning, holds them more accountable for their learning, and is therefore potentially more motivating for students than traditional grading
- It naturally promotes a knowledge construction approach to instruction rather than a simple information retention approach

With progress-based scoring it's *not* the student's level of attainment (e.g., A-B-C-D-E or 4-3-2-1 or Exceeds Expectations-Meets Expectations-Below Expectations-Needs Help) that is reported. It's the number of criteria per standard in which the accumulated work in their portfolio shows they have progressed or at least sustained their competence that gets reported.

Standards-Based, Progress-Based, Scoring and Reporting
With this process there is ...

- more student accountability (students must continue to show progress {growth} in order to score, they know exactly what they need to do to continue to show progress, and it is their responsibility to take advantage of every opportunity afforded them to keep growing)

- more teacher accountability (the rubric's criteria and bench-marks hold teachers accountable for providing students multiple opportunities to keep growing)
- more student empowerment (they get to be involved in self-assessment, take control of their own learning, and monitor their own learning/growth)
- measuring learning (monitoring their growing knowledge construct rather than subjectively trying to summate their ever-evolving knowledge construct)
- motivating learning (scores are at least as motivating as grades; progress grades (achievement) and knowing that progress is achievable are more motivating than final summative grades based on whether or not a norm was attained; *"I can make progress, even if it's just a little at a time."* vs. *"I try my hardest but don't ever reach the prized norm, so what's the use?!"*
- differentiated assessment which naturally promotes differentiated instruction
- alignment with what constructivist learning theory has revealed about learners and learning
- equity (every teacher is working from and toward the same power standards, the same criteria that comprise those standards, and from common rubrics for those standards, subsequently helping to ensure that every student is not only getting equal exposure to critical skills and knowledge but also being as objectively assessed as possible)

With this process there is *no*:

- need for proficiency labels (e.g., 4-3-2-1, Beyond Standard-At Standard-, etc.) on either the report card or the progress rubrics ... a simple arrow across the top of the rubric reflecting direction of growth is all that's needed
- use of cut-score grading scales (it's not the proficiency label {see above} under which the student falls that gets reported,

it's the number of the standard's criteria in which the student made progress that gets reported

- grading (no grading, just scoring ... scoring is more informative than grading, is criterion-referenced rather than norm-referenced, and does not discriminate against children)
- composite grading (no combining things like effort, participation, and neatness in with their acquisition of knowledge grade)... a separate score for each standard is given
- averaging of scores (averages don't reflect one's current knowledge anyway)
- weighting of assignments (eliminating one more unfair practice)
- giving or need to give zeros (see student accountability above) ... if work is not completed there is no zero given as punishment, the student simply does not get rewarded any progress
- need to grade students' work (true to standards-based teaching and learning it's the student's growth in the criteria of the standards that gets scored and reported, not their individual pieces of work and subsequent average of the grades they received on each of those pieces of work)
- student coasting (see student accountability above)
- need for progress reports to differ from report cards (report cards would simply be progress reports, as they should according to constructivist learning, because that is exactly what they would be reporting ... the student's progress)

This Scoring and Reporting System is Not Perfect

There aren't any out there that are. Though not perfect this approach helps perfect some key things pertaining to instruction and assessment.

It moves us to a more standards-based and less content/scope-and-sequence focused approach to instruction. It advances a more knowledge construction and less information recall approach to instruction and assessment, which in turn means more constructivist and less behaviorist classrooms.

It promotes more formative assessment and less evaluation (grading) and that means a greater focus on individualized progress versus comparative attainment by students. And last but definitely not least is it helps us come closer to our goal of ensuring greater and greater equity when it comes to reporting student learning.

And, in cases and places where the giving of grades is still required or desired this system will allow for even that to happen. Below is a sample of a standards-based, progress-based report card on which students' progress scores are converted into grades.

Student:	Angel			Date: December 20, 2008
Semester:	Fall			
Standard	Progress Score	Attainment Score	Grade P	Grade A
Meaning of Citizenship	5/6	1/6	A	D
Examines meaning of citizenship	2/2	1/2		
Debates meaning of citizenship	2/2	0/2		
Acts as a citizen	1/2	0/2		

The remaining power standards would be listed down the left hand column of the report card

Despite the discriminatory nature of grades and grading there remains demand for comparative, norm-referenced, attainment-based information. The "attainment score" on this report card meets that demand without having to resort to grades (see explanation below). However, to reiterate this key point one last time. If Angel had been graded the grades he would have received have been inserted off to the side of the report card. Looking at both sets of information, which of the four forms of reporting – progress score, attainment score, progress grade, attainment grade – is a) most likely to motivate students, b) most informative, c) most objective, d) most fair, and e) least discriminatory?

In this example, Meaning of Citizenship is one of the power standards in which Angel's progress is being reported. The report card lists below this standard its three criteria which are found on the VT Standard 6.9: Meaning of Citizenship progress rubric (see Section Four, Figure 1). There are two aspects of proficiency being measured for each of the three criteria, hence the denominator 2 for each criterion. Consequently, there are a total of six aspects of proficiency for this standard as a whole. The standard and its three criteria are copied right from the progress rubric for this standard, which students and parents would be familiar with prior to receiving this progress report/report card.

The "Progress Score" is the number of the standard's criteria in which Angel is demonstrating sustained progress at the time of reporting (5 out of 6), which Angel's most recently filled out progress rubric and accompanying work in his classroom formative assessment portfolio would evidence.

The "Attainment Score" is the number of the standard's criteria for which Angel has reached the third benchmark of progress on the progress rubric at the time of reporting (1 out of 6), which Angel's most recently completed progress rubric and accompanying work in his portfolio would show.

The "Grade" that has been added to the report solely for the purpose of this discussion is a norm-referenced, comparative measure of worth based on where Angel's performance falls on an arbitrarily decided (as they all are) cut-score grading scale. In this example the collaboratively agreed upon scale for all power standards with six criteria is 5-6 = A, 4 = B, 3 = C, 1-2 = D, 0 = F.

"Grade P" is the progress grade (Angel got an A) and "Grade A" is the attainment grade (Angel got a D). **Ouch!**

Four Keys to Going from Talking the Talk to Walking the Walk

1. Measuring student *progress* rather than student attainment
2. Using *progress* rubrics rather than just activity/task-specific rubrics or checklists

3. Scoring the students' ***progress*** rather than grading the students' work and subsequently the students themselves
4. Using the students' work to measure their ***growing*** understanding (knowledge construction, application, synthesis) rather than their retention of static information

~ VI ~

RESPONDING TO SKEPTICS AND CRITICS

"Aren't standards-based instruction and assessment and Mastery Learning the same thing?"

Some have tried to equate standards-based instruction and assessment with Mastery Learning. The two are substantially different and the critical difference between the two is this.

Mastery Learning tried to ensure that children learned particular content and skills *at the expense of moving them on in the curriculum.* Standards-based instruction ensures that children continually expand their proficiency in particular skills and content (i.e., the standards) by actually *moving through the curriculum.* In other words, where as in Mastery Learning children were **held back** until mastery, in standards-based instruction they are continually being **pushed forward.** They are continually working on the same standards but through continually changing contexts (content/units).

And so, two birds are being fed with one seed. Children receive exposure to a range of content while at the same time being given multiple opportunities to truly "master" the core essentials (the standards).

"What about quality?

"These progress rubrics don't measure the quality of the students' work. Isn't that important? How will we hold our students accountable for quality and effort if we aren't using rubrics that measure those attributes?"

Great question, great point, and ... that's exactly the point!

First, these progress rubrics measure six objective (objective, not subjective) aspects of proficiency. The work is either being done independently by the student or it isn't. Her work is either accurate or it's not, and it's either relevant to the information she's working from or it isn't. And frequency, amount, and span are all quantitative measures, not qualitative measures.

Given the high stakes nature of grading and how fallacious and flawed we now understand it to be, gone are the days of allowing someone (us) with a biased view judge (grade) a student's work ... with those grades, in turn, defining (labeling) the student, shaping the student's self-identity, self-worth, and self-esteem and ultimately regulating that student's opportunities in life both in and out of school, now and into the future.

And second, both quality and effort are being accounted for. Quality is typically embedded in the language of each criterion listed down the left hand side of the rubric. Effort is embedded in the ongoing process of standards-based formative instruction, assessment, scoring, and reporting. In order for a student to continue to progress across the rubric the student needs to continually show new and different evidence that she is continuing to grow or at least sustain her competency in the criteria in which she's being assessed. That takes effort.

"Assessing progress is nice but what about attainment? Isn't that important?!"

"I mean, if I need to have heart surgery I want to know that the doctor who's going to cut me open has attained the necessary degree of proficiency required to do heart surgery. I wouldn't want someone who is just making good progress be the one to cut me open! Attainment is important. And

isn't it the students' grades that sort out for us who have attained and who haven't?"

First, let's remember that in order to get to the so-called "attainment" level a person has to progress toward it. Progress cannot and should not be ignored.

Secondly, let's connect what we've learned about formative assessment versus summative evaluation to the scenario above. The doctor is in the position of performing heart surgery because she has proven time and time again, by way of multiple performance assessments, that she is capable of reliably, consistently, and independently performing heart surgery. *Ongoing, triangulated formative assessment of her work in the standards of heart surgery revealed at what point she had "attained" those standards, and her consequent license is simply a "summative certification" of that achievement.*

The same should be true for our students. If we need to know that a student has "attained" a certain skill (i.e., is "At Standard"), as opposed to being satisfied knowing that the student is making steady progress in the skill, it is the student's classroom formative assessment portfolio and accompanying progress rubrics and not his grades (grades being what we typically use as a summative certification of a student) that verify for us just exactly which skills he is "At Standard" in and which he is not. In addition, for those skills he has not yet attained the progress rubrics tell us exactly what degree of attainment he has achieved. And it is this idea of varying degrees of attainment which leads to what is really the deeper discussion around the issues of "attainment," especially grading based on "attainment."

"Education is not the filling of a bucket but the lighting of a fire." (Yeats)

"When the student is ready the master appears." (Japanese Proverb)

"Teachers open the door but you must enter by yourself." (Chinese Proverb)

Our responsibility as teachers is to continually engage our students in individualized, developmentally appropriate opportunities that promote their progress toward eventual "attainment" of the standards. That is what is in our control. What is not totally within our control is the degree to which those students engage in those multiple enabling activities and the rate at which each individual is able to progress toward meeting those standards. That is affected by a host of identifiable and unidentifiable variables ranging from physiological, emotional to cultural. We cannot control when and if our students truly attain. All we can do is monitor and measure their individual progress and continue to instruct accordingly (i.e., formatively assess and instruct).

In addition, "attainment" itself is an illusion, hence the quotation marks. Ecology, constructivism, and phenomenology reveal that everything is in a constant state of evolution and everything is infinitely nested. In other words, nothing is static and nothing is finite. There is always another level, layer, or degree. Hence, there is no finality in learning and therefore *true attainment* is unobtainable. So any time we set a standard that we hope our students will attain, all we are doing is simply setting and defining a level of proficiency that we believe is "good enough." We are simply marking a "finish" line at an arbitrary point along an eternal course of **progress**.

Having standards to work toward is a constructive and worthwhile practice. However, it is crucial we remember that those standards are subjective, assessing attainment of those standards is extremely interpretive, and true attainment of them is impossible to pinpoint. And no matter what the standards, children will, for legitimate reasons many of which are out of their control, progress toward attainment of those standards at different rates.

Finally, as implied in the quote at the top of this essay, assessing and ultimately evaluating (grading) students based on progress does not inhibit or prohibit students from attainment nor does it keep us from knowing and being able to proclaim when students "attain" (i.e., have reached our agreed-upon "good enough" level of proficiency) certain skills and standards. The standards-based progress rubrics that we work from and toward as we guide our students toward attainment of those standards allow us to assess our students' progress and "attainment" simultaneously.

The issue isn't whether we should or shouldn't be concerned with attainment. The issues are whether we should be grading students based on "attainment" as opposed to grading them based on their progress, and whether grades are in any way a reflection of attainment. Given our understanding of "attainment" and the numerous validity and reliability issues that surround grading, shouldn't attainment-based grading be abolished?

"But aren't we supposed to be preparing students to succeed at the next level?"

"If we assess and subsequently evaluate students just based on their individual progress what happens if they don't acquire the skills they need in order to succeed at the next grade level? Don't we have a responsibility to make sure they know and can do certain things before they move on to the next grade level?"

First, it's important to acknowledge some of the assumptions that underlie the above concern. The first is that there are certain givens that every child can and must possess upon leaving one grade level and moving on to the next. A second is that those givens have been determined in a valid, reliable, and fair way by an objective authority. A third is that those givens are fair "zones of proximal development" (Vygotsky, 1978) for each individual's learning and development curve. A possible fourth is that if students are not held accountable to externally imposed expectations of attainment they will not be motivated to put forth sustained effort to progress with their learning.

Given that learning is a constructivist process and that we learn at different rates, in different ways, and in varying and unpredictable leaps, spurts, fits, and starts, if prerequisite skills are to exist some questions worth reflecting on include:

- Does constructivist learning support the existence of grade levels?
- Does it support having set, scheduled increments of attainment?
- If expectations do exist are they developmentally appropriate for every student?
- Were the many cultural and developmental factors (most being outside of the child's control) that have impacted and continue to impact each individual's learning and development curves considered when those expectations were determined?
- Are those prerequisites student-centered or are they teacher-, curriculum-, and/or external accountability-centered?
- Aren't prerequisite skills and grade level expectations simply norms?

Grade level expectations and prerequisite skills are essentially norms. If grades are based on achievement of grade level expectations then what exists is a norm-referenced grading system. Consequently, when students are graded on whether or not they are able to attain grade level expectations they are receiving norm-referenced grades. Students who are able to attain someone's biased idea of what a student should know and be able to do at their respective grade level receive A's. Students who are unable to achieve that level receive something less than an A. What results is a grade report that ranks students against one another based on their ability to meet someone's phenomenological view of what is important and when it's important. In other words, students who happen to fit the desired mold are being rewarded. Those who don't are being punished.

On the contrary, assessing and grading students based on their individual progress toward meeting collaboratively agreed-upon "good enough" levels of proficiency in the standards is a purely criterion-referenced process that in no way interferes with students attaining grade level expectations if they exist. In fact, the individualized focus on what the students can do as opposed to what they can't do motivates students to succeed.

The progress students make toward "proficiency" and whether they reach those levels within set periods of time (e.g., a marking period, a school year) depends on the prior knowledge and experience they come to class with, the interplay of the many developmental and cultural factors that influence their motivation and learning curves, and the differentially-responsive multiple opportunities being provided for them by the teacher accordingly. Grading them on progress does not preclude teachers from meeting their responsibility to give their students every opportunity and every tool they need in order to succeed. *And it is these things, not grading based on attainment, which impact whether students "attain" grade level expectations.*

And finally, assessing and ultimately grading (if necessary) students based on progress, as opposed to attainment, does not preclude teachers from having prerequisites, goals, objectives, outcomes, criteria, standards, essential understandings, or expectations of attainment. These are all important for both the teacher and student to have and to work from and toward. Attainment of them, however, should never be the basis on which a child is evaluated (graded).

"But grades are a motivator!"

There is some evidence that grades are a constructive motivator for some students. What is not clear, however, is whether those grades are motivating the student to want to learn or motivating her simply because she desires the affirmation of success (praise, reward) good grades bring her. And if it's the latter students are seeking, that can easily be provided in ways other than grades.

There is substantial evidence that grades are not a constructive motivator for most students. If they *are* motivating they tend to motivating in a punitive rather than positive way, spurring students to comply in order to avoid the many negative consequences and loss of privileges that come with bad grades.

And finally, if grades are not motivating students to learn, or at least complete their work, the natural consequence is not to fail them but simply to not reward them.

Grades and Motivation, Take Two

One reason often stated in support for grading students is that grades are a motivator. But just how true is that? Let's consider the following.

First, why are we finding ourselves in the situation of having to motivate students to learn in the first place? Humans are innately curious organisms biochemically wired to desire learning. Watch any young child at play, or when children first come to school. Think of yourselves when you decided to take on a new hobby or wanted to further explore something you heard on the news. Did you need to know you were going to be graded before pursuing that new learning? Did you need extrinsic motivators of any kind? What is going on that by third grade or so we feel we have to resort to extrinsic motivators (grades) to get students to do something that's intrinsic? Or do we?

Second, is it true grades motivate students to learn? Is the grade motivating them to learn? *Or is it motivating them to comply*? And is it the grade that is increasing student learning? Or is it student engagement that contributes to increased learning? Some argue that the grade motivates the student to engage and so that yes, indirectly the grade is increasing student learning. Others argue that even if all the grade is doing is forcing them to comply, if by complying they increase their learning then so be it. These sentiments lead to a third consideration.

If the grade is a true motivator is it a positive or negative motivator? In other words, are students truly being motivated to want to learn more and more because they're being graded, or are they putting forth effort to "learn" so as to avoid the punitive consequences of bad grades such as being labeled, damage to self-esteem, punishment, loss of privileges, loss of opportunities, etc.?

Research shows that for some students who are already motivated to do well in school grades can serve as an additional motivator. For everyone else grades have been shown to be a non-motivator.

And finally, if after this conversation one still feels grades are a worthy motivator, the question to ask next is, "Ok, but why not simply use scores as your motivator rather than discriminatory grades?"

"But employers (society) want and need to know who's capable and competent!"

Employers don't want grades. They want to know exactly what the person actually knows and is able to do relevant to their workplace. And, as we know, at best grades only reflect one very narrow and temporal aspect of one's overall capability and competency.

Old Assumptions and Tired Arguments

It is commonly assumed that we need to grade students because society (colleges, employers) needs some way to know who is capable and who is not. It is also commonly assumed that "good" students get high grades and "poor" students get low grades. In turn, "good" students are assumed to be hard working, "smart," and quick, and "poor" students are assumed to be slow, not too "smart," and unmotivated. Consequently, it is assumed that grades reflect general intelligence and work ethic, and in our society, aside from wealth and who you know, presumed intelligence and work ethic govern who gets their foot in the door.

However, there are two serious flaws in these assumptions ... one pertaining to grading itself and the other to the notion that good students equate to good prospects. When we analyze the mechanics (averaging, weighting, composite grading, giving zeros, using cut-score grading scales) and embedded biases (bias over quality of work and effort, bias over what should count and be graded, etc.) of grading we quickly expose it for what it is … invalid, unreliable, unfair, and seriously flawed. And … "good" students are not necessarily good employees and vice versa, a fact regularly reported by post-secondary schools.

So given all this, some recent campaign slogans are quite timely. "It's time for change," and "Yes we can!"

"But this is the real world! Isn't it our responsibility to prepare kids for that?!"

Prepare them to be graded? Or prepare them to succeed in life? Yes, it is absolutely our responsibility to help prepare kids to succeed once they leave school. And yes, competition is a part of the yin and yang of competition and cooperation that sustains all systems. But the connection proponents of the "It's the real world" argument make between the competitive market, the "real world," and grading students deserves scrutiny.

Yes, employers do "evaluate" their employees' job performance, and thankfully so. But in how many jobs that you know of do they use a "one-time-frame-fits-all" comparative grading approach to do so?

Let's look at teaching for example. How many of you are in a school or district where you are all given the same set of skills to grow in within a set time frame and then at the conclusion of that time period your personal rate of growth is placed within a common, normed cut-score scale and *comparatively* ranked?!

But this is exactly what we do to our students semester after semester, year after year.

And we're guilty of further hypocrisy. Just look at our own general outcry over schools and teachers being judged ("graded") based on their students' test results.

The way to prepare kids for the "real world" is to explain to them how competition works in partnership with cooperation and to promote in them a passion for wanting to continually grow their knowledge and skills.

"Real World," Take Two

Absolutely! It is our responsibility to help prepare kids to succeed once they leave school. And yes, competition is a part of the real world yin and yang of competition alongside cooperation that sustains all systems. But the connection that proponents of the "real world" argument make between competition, the "real world," and grades warrants questioning. Aside from all the validity and reliability issues we now understand around grading, grades do not inform us as to exactly what one knows and is able to do. And, those with the highest grades are a) not necessarily more competent, and b) might not even be proficient, just simply more competent than those with lower grades.

The heart surgeon discussion earlier is a start to this discourse. Yes, employers do assess their employees' job performance and thankfully so. But in how many jobs that you know of do they discriminatorily grade them?

The way to prepare kids for the real world is to explain to them how competition works hand-in-hand with cooperation and promote in them positive motivation to want to continually grow, make progress, and improve their knowledge and skills so they can be successful. And as we've seen during this workshop there is a fair and valid way to do that that does not require discriminatorily grading them.

"But won't this process of grading students on their individual progress lead to higher grades and a lot more A's?"

If grade inflation is a concern for someone, that suggests they hold the following underlying beliefs and assumptions. First, schooling is meant to be a selective process where students are to be comparatively ranked, sorted, and culled. Second, students, rather than be rewarded for achievement, should be rewarded for *relative* achievement ... either relative to others or relative to norms (commonly accepted levels of achievement which are inevitably and inherently culturally and/or developmentally biased). Third, students may or may not be able to learn equally within the same time period but whether they can or can't doesn't matter. And fourth, grades *are* objective, valid, and reliable measures that accurately reflect what students actually know and are able to do.

Grade Inflation, Take Two

Grade inflation is a concern for those whose underlying beliefs include 1) schooling is meant to be a selective process, 2) students need to be graded not based on success but on relative success ... either relative to others or to norms (commonly accepted levels of achievement which are inevitably and inherently culturally and developmentally biased), and 3) grades can be objectively derived and are valid and reliable categorizations that truly reflect the relative abilities of their students.

"But wait! A kid who makes a lot of progress and a kid who only makes a little progress can both get A's?!"

First, it's important to remind people that with this system there should not be any grades involved and consequently this concern is moot.

If, however, you are in a system which requires that grades be given, and that your students' progress scores at reporting time have to be converted to grades, then yes, this scenario is absolutely possible. And what *if* every student gets an A? *Why is that a problem?* From a teacher's standpoint it would be a tremendous thing if every single student succeeded. That would be something worth celebrating. Isn't seeing kids learn, grow, mature, succeed, and feel great about themselves the reason we wanted to be teachers in the first place?

It's also worth noting what underlies this concern ... a certain orientation around the concept of competition. There is a time and place for competition, just as there is a time and place for cooperation and collaboration. Systems theory reveals that in sustainable systems cooperation is more at work than competition. Those who express the above concern, however, have a deep rooted belief in the supremacy of competition, and that competition not only has a place in school but that it should underlie and drive how schooling is done. In other words they have adopted the notion that school should be a selective enterprise through which children are sorted, ranked, and culled.

It is critically important that those who hold this belief recognize it because if this is their core principle there is no way it is not affecting how they interact with individual students, and how they teach. Teaching from a competitive orientation looks very different than teaching from a collaborative orientation. For starters, it tends to be more about the teacher and teacher control, and less about the students.

And yes, if we replace the "...can both get A's?!" in the quote above to "... can both get the same score?!" that, too, can happen with this system. And again, why is that a problem?

After all, grades do not, never have, and never will accurately reflect what a student knows and is able to do. And scores won't either. The only thing that shows us what a student knows and is able to do is the student's classroom formative assessment portfolio and accompanying progress rubrics. But at least with scores there are no theoretical fallacies, technical flaws, and blatant discrimination occurring, as is the case with grades and grading.

Scores are one small step for students and one giant leap for social justice. A *giant step* for students would then be to move away from scores and simply allow their standards-based progress rubrics become their report card.

"Isn't progress scoring open to kids underachieving?"
When this concern is expressed it is commonly around two particular scenarios. One is kids deliberately marking themselves low

on their initial baseline assessment if that initial assessment is a self-assessment, and two, kids doing as little as they have to knowing they'll still get credit for making progress or at least sustaining their competency.

First, it is important to recognize that for us to even have these concerns means we are already experiencing these underachieving behaviors from our students. In other words, underachievement is happening now with the system we are currently using. So what do we have to lose giving this system and honest try? And isn't it our professional (and personal?) responsibility to give this approach a try knowing all the theoretical, technical, and ethical flaws of our current approach to reporting student learning?

Second, it is worth questioning just how many students would actually demonstrate this behavior. Children are naturally curious and inquisitive. They are innate learners. As well, they have an innate drive to succeed. If they do get to a point in school where they choose to underachieve, would the cause of that be this approach to reporting their learning or is there something else about school, or elsewhere, that is promoting that behavior?

Back to the two scenarios stated earlier. If a student does deliberately mark herself low on her initial self-assessment technically it will not matter. From that point on the only way she can get credit for making progress, or at least sustaining her competency, is to provide new evidence ... new and different from the evidence that was looked at the last time she was marked on the rubric. And if she doesn't produce any new evidence, that will not only be evident in her portfolio but reflected in where she is able to land on her accompanying progress rubric at that time.

Scenario two is students only doing the bare minimum knowing all they have to do is show progress. As in scenario one the fact that they have to produce new evidence all along the way, combined with use of a well-constructed standards-based progress rubric, makes getting credit for minimal effort virtually impossible. Given that it's the standards (for which there is no finality in growth) rather than content students are being assessed in, and it is progress rubrics rather than an attainment measuring rubrics being used to monitor their learning, students cannot get away with minimal effort if they want to get credit for their work.

I say "virtually" impossible because, as with anything in life, nothing is full proof and there are always exceptions. If a case arises where, despite using a well-designed standards-based progress rubric, somehow a student is able to show well on the rubric despite little or no effort ... two things. First, as with any reporting system it's not the grade or score that comprehensively reflect what a student knows and is able to do, it's their actual work. The student's classroom formative assessment portfolio will reveal if she's chosen to do minimal work. Second, on a progress rubric there is always a comment section. If a student has somehow progressed or maintained their place on the rubric despite giving little or no effort simply state that in the comment section on the rubric and report card. But if that does happen, check the reliability of the rubric being used.

And finally, related to the notion of underachieving is concern over students not bothering to complete work. Is our current approach of threatening and punishing students in order to pry work out of them really promoting their work ethic and sense of responsibility? Or would an approach based on natural consequences be more apt to not only promote those sensibilities but gradually have them become more intrinsic.

With true progress scoring no work means no new evidence is being provided. No new evidence means there can be no progress or sustained competency, which in turn means regressing on the rubric. The consequences that result from regressing on the rubric are just that ... natural.

"What about high schools?

"Aren't we going to be doing our students a disservice with this approach? What happens when they go to high school where their grades are going to be based on their attainment?"

Standards-based, criterion-referenced, formative instruction, assessment, and reporting is more an alternative approach to grading than it is instruction. With this approach students will still be exposed to rich content (arguably richer than in a traditional scope-and-sequence curriculum because this approach focuses on knowledge construction rather than information retention) and opportunities to become familiar with and hone their skills in methods typically used at the high school level ... methods such as reading textbooks, answering questions at the end of chapters in those texts, and taking traditional quizzes and tests. In other words, with this approach the teacher can still expose her students to the same types of activities she knows they are going to experience in high school, the difference being that she is simply using those activities as formative assessments rather than summative evaluations. She won't be any less able to prepare her students for high school than she was when she was doing content-based, norm-referenced grading and reporting.

"Just because progress scoring rather than grading works for us doesn't mean it will work for them. It works for us because we're independent and motivated learners."

And so are students ... at least when they first come to school.

Yes, this approach does work for adult learners. We know it also works for elementary students who have not yet been subjected to traditional grading, know only qualitative feedback, and are generally still intrinsically motivated to do well despite what their report card says. And we also know it can work at the middle school level. Everything that has been presented here originates from three years of standards-based progress scoring in a middle school classroom.

For the concern above to even exist it means two things. First, we know what independent and motivated learners look like *and we know what students who don't fit that description look like.* Second, for us to know that means we are already experiencing both types of students. ***In other words, this is already a problem with our current approach to "schooling."*** That, alone, is justification for us to give this approach an honest try. Some would argue that given what we know about the theoretical, technical, and ethical flaws of our current approach to grading it is our professional (and personal?) responsibility to give it a try.

The concern expressed above most often comes from teachers of older students. And the more we hear it the more we are left with the impression that high school teaching is more like a daily power struggle with students than a stimulating and fulfilling team experience of mutual learning.

We've discussed how high school students do typically have the hardest time with adjusting to progress scoring because all they've known since third grade or so is grading, and that what counts is the grade and not necessarily what has been learned. But today's adults (you and I for example) share that same history with grading. So if this approach works for us and for pre-high school students then why can't it work for high school students?

"What about Honor Roll?"

Honor Roll, AP classes, Dean's List, promotion, and grades in general all rely on cut-score scales but the sorting and ranking that results doesn't distinguish students as it's assumed to do, it discriminates against many of them. How?

Grades are generally assumed to be a reflection of "intelligence." But when we consider 1) the technical flaws inherent in the way grades are concocted (e.g., averaging, weighting, etc.), 2) the inconsistency from teacher to teacher as to what is actually getting graded (information retention, knowledge construction, short-term memory, effort, higher level thinking skills, alternative thinking, facts, concepts, skills, participation, following directions, etc. etc.), and 3) the inconsistency from teacher to teacher as to what does and doesn't qualify as good ("A") work, we quickly uncover that grades invariably reflect everything and anything ... and perhaps nothing at all with respect to a student's "intelligence."

Grades never have and never will tell us exactly what a student actually knows and is able to do. The grade doesn't tell us that, it's the student's classroom formative assessment portfolio and accompanying progress rubrics that clearly show us that.

So ... back to honor roll. The only thing we know for sure about students who did or didn't make honor roll is that those who did were able to succeed with their teacher's curriculum and make his subjective cut within the time frame he happened to give them to do it in, and those who didn't were simply unable to succeed with *their* teacher's curriculum and/or make *her* cut within the time frame *she* set. And as we saw above and all know, that variability in teachers' curricula and expectations (i.e., inequity) does exist.

This, then, brings us back to what constructivism tells us about how learning occurs and how attainment-based norm-referencing is antithetical to what we know. Grading and honor roll simply favor the former student described in the previous paragraph and discriminates against the latter.

Undoubtedly no one disagrees with the idea of recognizing student achievement and honoring students accordingly. And that is the well-intended notion behind the concept of an honor roll. But because an honor roll automatically relies on a cut-score grading scale, and therefore attainment-based norm-referencing, it will automatically be discriminatory.

If we acknowledge this but decide to still have an honor roll then it is imperative we make it as less discriminatory and more distinguishing as we possibly can. The formative, progress-based criterion-referenced approach we've been exploring allows us to take a huge step in that direction. Although it would still require use of a cut-score scale, that single honor roll cut-score would be the only cut-score used throughout the entire process and therefore the only discriminatory step in the grading process. Here's how it would work.

If every teacher is 1) working from and toward a common set of power standards, 2) using common rubrics for each of those power standards (everyone would also be working from and toward a consistent set of criteria and benchmarks), and 3) simply scoring* their students as opposed to grading them (i.e., simply monitoring the number of criteria per standard in which each student has either made progress or at least sustained their competency and representing that growth as a score only** (e.g., Respect – 1/2; Scientific Method – 12/16, etc.) then all that everyone needs to do next is to collaboratively agree upon what they believe is a reasonable honor roll cut-score.

For example, if everyone is working from and toward 20 power standards, which combined have a total of 60 criteria, they might decide that a reasonable cut-score might be 45. Any student who, at the time of reporting (report card time), has demonstrated he/she has either made progress in or at least worked to sustain their competency in at least 45 of the 60 criteria would be entitled to be on the honor roll.

Again, from a constructivist learning standpoint this would still be a discriminatory practice. Just as there are uncontrollable and legitimate reasons why some people are able to learn some things well and other things not so well and why some people learn faster than others (see "Trees Diagram, Section Three), so too are there legitimate reasons why at times any one of us might not be able to make even the slightest progress. So although this approach to honor roll is still discriminatory it is far less flawed than the way grading and honor roll are conventionally being done.

*Scores are simply direct quantitative representations of actual achievement (e.g., ten correct out of twelve would be a score of 10/ 12, progress in three of the standard's four criteria would be a score of 3/4). When those scores are then categorized by way of any form of cut-score grading scale they have then gone from being scores to now being grades (e.g., 10/12-12/12=A, 8/12-9/12=B, etc. or 3/4 criteria=At Standard, 2/4 criteria=Almost There, 1/4 criteria=Good Start).

** Ideally, teams of teachers will be collaboratively assessing student work in those 60 criteria and agreeing on where the student is on the accompanying rubrics (i.e., collaborative assessment of student learning {CASL}) so that when report card time rolls around and it's time to tally a student's score, that score is a collaboratively agreed-upon score rather than a single teacher's opinion, the latter of which is always more subjective than the former.

"What about colleges?

"Isn't this going to put our students at a disadvantage for getting into college if colleges want grades?"

One interesting thing to consider relative to this question is home schooling. Home schooled children are getting into colleges as are students coming from non-graded schools.

Many colleges have begun to change their admissions requirements perhaps primarily because of three major acknowledgments. First, those in education, including admissions personnel, have long known that grades are extremely subjective and arbitrary. Student performance that earns an A from Teacher 1 or School X would very likely have earned something different from Teacher 2 or School Y.

A second acknowledgment is the steadily escalating phenomenon of grade inflation. For many reasons, perhaps mostly political, students' grades have generally been on the rise over the past decade. Greater proportions of students graduating from high school are coming out with high GPA's. And yet, when these students come to college, professors continually bemoan the fact that these so-called "good students" are woefully ill-prepared for college.

The third is the recognition that grades are not a valid reflection of what a student knows and is able to do, and that grades are often heavily determined by test results. Educators recognize that there are many dimensions to a student's intelligence and ability, and that no one evaluation tool can capture the whole picture. In other words, there is recognition that more formative, portfolio-like data is required if one is to have a true picture of a student's proficiency and potential. Many schools are moving to a more portfolio-like admissions process and many are choosing to no longer rely as heavily on, and in many cases not rely on at all, quantitative data such as GPA, class rank, and standardized test results. That growing list of colleges can be found at www.fairtest.org-optlistPDF.pdf.

"Listen! One plus one is two. It just is. So what's wrong with grading kids based on whether they got the answer right or not?"

"School taught one and one is two. But right now that answer just ain't true."

(Ride My Seesaw, Moody Blues, 1968)

The theoretical, technical, and ethical fallacies of grading we've been exploring are arguably justification for the "...what's wrong with grading kids ..." portion of the quote above, whether they get the answer right or not, or for any other reason. There is a lot wrong with it.

With regard to the "... it just is ..." portion of the quote, with post-modern revelation that the whole is greater than the sum of its parts, even the presumed truth that one and one is two is challenged. But whether one and one is two or not isn't the primary issue here. What the above sentiment incites, in addition to discourse over grading and whether there really are right and wrong answers, is debate over what is education.

Is education about instilling in children what is commonly accepted as fact ("truth")? Or is it more about encouraging them to continually question and challenge what is commonly accepted as right?

As educators we generally agree we want our students to think critically, take risks, and think alternatively ... to think "outside the box" and to think in ways that will result in change for the better ... like those who asked the following ...

Are natural resources really limitless commodities free for us to exploit? Are you sure there aren't principles of ecology we need to understand and an environmental ethic we'd be better off abiding to?

Are you sure that children are just miniature versions of adults who come to the classroom with a mind and brain that are a "blank slate?" Isn't there something more to how humans learn, which anyone who teaches would do well to know?

Are we sure women and black Americans can't be entrusted with the right to vote? Might not their collective participation in the democratic process actually benefit all of us?

One "truth," at least for now, is that everything is in a formative (shaping while at the same time being shaped) state ... continually adapting, (co)evolving, and transforming. It can't be helped. Perpetual change happens.

And aren't those who question "truth" the ones who contribute most toward new learning and constructive transformation? There are many, many more examples of presumed right answers like the three above that someone dared to topple, and in so doing ultimately brought about change for the better. Shouldn't education be not just about providing students with presumed right answers but also continually encouraging them to then question and challenge those "right" answers?

Are We Now in an Ethical Dilemma?

Teachers have to grade their students, for now anyway, but thanks to lead teachers like you change is coming.

Some of us have to say whether our students are "A" students or "less than A" students. Others have to say whether our students are "4" students or "less than 4" students. And still others have to say whether our students are "At Standard" or "Proficient" students or "less than At Standard" or "less than Proficient" students.

The ways in which we are concocting those grades include practices such as averaging, weighting, composite grading, giving zeros, grading some assignments but not others, dropping some grades but keeping others, and using an arbitrary hodgepodge of different types of cut-score grading scales (e.g., pre-determined, post-determined, fixed traditional, adjusted, normal distribution, etc.). And far too often our final decisions on our students' grades are based on our subjective opinion influenced by our biases ... which means based on some degree of guesswork.

As we've uncovered, every one of these practices is deeply flawed. And if these practices are deeply flawed then so are the grades we're giving our students. If we know this is this not a moral dilemma for us? Isn't it our responsibility to stop doing something we know is wrong, even if other stakeholders still want it to continue?

If we truly are under the oppression of some systemic constraint (e.g., mandatory grading policies, type of report card, electronic grading software) that we truly can't change ... but wait a minute! Change is natural. Everything is in a constant state of change. Nothing is static. So what makes the systemic constraint we claim is holding us hostage so special and resistant to natural law? Why can't it be changed? If we truly can't change it, if we know it's seriously flawed shouldn't we at least be chipping away at it by improving upon it in any way we possibly can?

By applying this system of standards-based, progress-based instruction, assessment, scoring and reporting, to whatever degree you are able, you will be making substantial improvements over what's currently taking place. And in time, as your approach takes hold from within, it will force those seemingly immovable objects (mandatory grading policies, report cards, electronic grade books) to shift ... and eventually topple. And as with any change it will be slow and painful. But knowing it is allowing us to be more respectful to our students is what's going to help us hang in there during this transformation.

~ VII ~

AFTERWORD

Phenomenology and Grading

When someone receives an A the A suggests the person either is the best or did the best. It suggests they are better than those who received less than an A. But is it really true that they are the best or did the best? Our exploration of the technical flaws of grading (averaging, weighting, composite grading, giving zeros, use of discriminatory cut-score grading scales) and the ways in which grading is antithetical to constructivist learning theory has left us questioning this assumption. A look at phenomenology gives us pause as well.

Employer:"Yeah, sure, she's got a college degree in this field but reality is she's completely incompetent!" (Reality for the college was she was competent. Are they both right?)

College:"Yeah, sure, he was a straight A student in high school but reality is he doesn't know anything!" (Reality for the school was he was knowledgeable. Are they both right?)

Our "best" students are going to encounter many people throughout their lives who are not going to think they or their work are the best even if they are at their personal best. And what's considered "best" now, in time, will not be what's considered best. "Best" is fleeting and that is a natural phenomenon. And therefore the stigma of an A is fleeting as well. Nothing is static. Everything is in a constant state of evolution, change, and transformation. It's arguable that "best," in its most literal sense, cannot ever truly exist. At best (excuse the pun) it is a temporally circumstantial, contextually relative perception or appearance of being. It is momentary and specific to a select context (time and space). And so any sorting, ranking, categorizing, and grading we do is also temporally circumstantial and context-specific.

We have already uncovered how grades and grading are antithetical to just about everything we know, understand, and believe about children and teaching and learning. Grades are antithetical to theory as well. Systems theory points out that contrary to learning grades are static, non-constructive, and non-evolving. Ecology reveals that grades demote and discourage diversity. Constructivism and cognitive science expose that given what we now know about learning, knowledge construction, and schema development grades and grading are discriminatory. And phenomenology reveals grades are relativistic and illusory.

When we grade (use cut-score grading scales and categorize) students we, perhaps unwittingly but nonetheless naturally, factor out the multitude of varying social, cultural, physiological, and psychological variables promoting or inhibiting our students' learning and that account for the varying levels of readiness, zones of proximal development, and learning curves that exist among our students at the time those grades are given.

Grading is an attempt to judge (evaluate) one's state of learning. It is an attempt to categorize and place a fixed value on one's construct of knowledge ... a construct that is perpetually fluid and in a continual state of construction, deconstruction, and reconstruction. Therefore, any grade given is an instantly (literally within seconds) obsolete categorization of worth.

And finally, grading is about finality. Grades are final but there is no finality in learning. Though a student's learning continues and her knowledge construct is forever expanding, not one of the obsolete grades she receives along the way ever goes away. They are final. Grade books, averaging, and report cards all permanently fix grades, not just in written records but mental records as well.

Grading is the highest stakes thing we do in education. Grades regulate opportunity for children, both in and out of school, starting with the very first grade they receive. Given all we now know and understand about grades and grading should grading be a practice we want to continue imposing on students?

Dear Mr. Illich

In his book, *Deschooling Society* (1970), Ivan Illich discusses the fallacy of "school." Isn't it time we concede he was right? School reform has been constant throughout the century surrounding his book. Yet despite all of that reformation, *trans*formation of schools continues to elude us. Why is that?

Over the past twenty years, both as a public school and graduate education teacher, I have gone from being curious about Illich's work, to regularly citing him, to essentially becoming an "Ivanista." Certain aspects of schooling, grading for one, have always felt suspect to me. But over the years the inherent fallacy of "school" itself has become undeniable.

The endless waves of reform we have witnessed over the decades, for the most part, have been well intended. Recent initiatives such as differentiated instruction and doing away with grading are soundly in line with what cognitive science has revealed about learning. Unfortunately, replacing traditional education practices with progressive ones has been analogous to simply replacing random bricks in an otherwise monolithic "brick wall."

To try and understand why this is we have to start by looking at systems. Systems are inherently progressive because they are governed by formative processes. They are never static, but instead continually evolving. External influences constantly push systems to internally reorganize themselves. In turn, reorganized systems then reshape those external forces that reshaped them, and so on.

With "school," however, we often witness reorganization under external pressure, *but rarely if ever do we see the reciprocal effect.* There are two key reasons for this. First, "school" is inherently conservative. Schools preserve the past. Students learn knowledge and develop skills that are already part of, and that simply self-perpetuate the human experience *as we can only know it.*

Second is the notion of "teacher." Hopefully those who are teaching our children are lifelong learners who continually keep up with the latest research and information not just in the subject area they teach but in their field in general. Consequently, what they teach their students is relevant, and the way in which they teach is through what's currently believed to be best practice.

However, no matter how current teachers are they can't sever themselves from their past. What they learned years ago, and how they were schooled, not only shaped but continue to shape their understanding of the world and the way they teach. Any information they assimilate, accommodate, and hopefully transform is still an offshoot of their roots. And so, even the most progressive teacher still conserves the status quo to some degree.

To compound this, the typical teacher who comes into the field is a recent graduate from a school of education ... a school about school *as we know it.* The courses they took to get their teaching certificates consisted of the same classical subjects they experienced in school, and education theory and methods courses that provided them with little actual experience in the world of teaching. And the instructors they had for these courses all had similar courses during their training. Walk into any classroom today and with the exceptions of technology and perhaps more recent history being covered, what you typically experience is a classroom not all that different from when you were a student.

There is plenty in the literature suggesting that education is perhaps the slowest field to evolve. But other fields are comprised of people with the same inseparable connection to their past. How is it that those fields are locked in a transformative spiral but schools are not?

Aside from school being inherently conservative this phenomenon is perpetuated by who becomes our teachers and how. Students who go into other fields such as business, technology, and medicine have a very similar K-12 experience as those who go on to become teachers. Then after high school they either go to college to specialize in the field of their choice or directly into the work world. In both cases those are worlds that are very different from what they experienced in school. Their existing knowledge is greatly perturbed as they are immersed in this new experience. And the more our schemas are perturbed the more they transform.

Students who go into teaching, on the other hand, leave high school and go on to a college experience relatively similar to their high school experience. After that, they go into a career they are already quite familiar with because they have spent almost their entire lives as students coexisting with teachers in a school setting. The amount of perturbation they experience is relatively minimal compared to those who go into other fields.

Not surprisingly, what they teach and how they teach is essentially the same as what they were taught and how they were taught ... not unlike what we witness when we see children playing school. Again, walk into a classroom today and you are bound to see the same fundamental skills and subject areas being taught, assignments being given, classroom management being practiced, and grading practices being used when you were a student.

Related to this is how compliance-oriented teachers tend to be. What I described above is partly to blame but it's also because schools are compliance-based institutions. Standards, grade level expectations, grades, discipline policies, and failure and promotion to name a few all come down to compliance. Behave, do what you need to do to get good grades and maintain your eligibility to participate in extra-curricular activities, be promoted to the next grade level, graduate and get a good job. That is what students come to know school as.

Observe the typical teacher in a graduate program and you will see their orientation toward compliance still, both as a student in the program and in their teaching.

One step to disrupt this cycle of reformation without transformation and compliance mindedness might be to mandate that teachers spend time in a field outside of education before they can be certified to teach. The extra perturbation that experience will exert on their world view will allow them to then return to school not as an "insider" who will simply conserve the status quo but as more of an "outsider" with a more worldly view ... a view that in turn will be a source of dissonance that will trigger evolution within the school itself. And as those other fields continually evolve, new teachers coming in with experience from those fields will in turn keep schools in an upward spiral of continuous transformation.

This proposal is not about recruiting subject matter experts from other professions to serve as teachers. Opponents of that practice, of which I am one, rightfully argue that knowledge of a discipline does not necessarily make one a good teacher. Rather, it is about ensuring that schools of education immerse potential teachers in constructivist learning theory, and then place them in work outside of education before allowing them to become teachers. By doing so, this will open them up to synthesize and apply their teacher education in a more progressive rather than conservative way. Until that happens teachers will continue to be preservers of the status quo and schools will look the same in the coming century as they do now, and have for the past century.

Additional Resources

Ainsworth, L. (2003). *Power standards: Identifying the standards that matter the most.* Englewood, CO: Advanced Learning Press.

Arter, J. & McTighe, J. (2000). *Scoring rubrics in the classroom.* Thousand Oaks, CA: Corwin Press.

Birman, B., Desimone, L., Porter, A., &Garet, M. (2000). Designing professional development that works. *Educational Leadership,* 57 (5), 28-33.

Black, P. & Wiliam, D. (1998). Inside the black box: Raising standards through classroom assessment. *Phi Delta Kappan,* October, 1998.

Blum, S. D. 2020. *Ungrading: Why rating students undermines learning (and what go do instead).* Morgantown, WV: West Virginia University Press.

Brookhart, S. *How to create and use rubrics for formative assessment and grading.* Alexandria, VA: ASCD.

___ (2009). *Grading.* New York, NY: Pearson.

___ (2008). *How to give effective feedback to your students.* Alexandria, VA: ASCD.

___(2004). Classroom Assessment: Tensions and intersections in theory and practice. *Teachers College Record,* 106(3), 429-458.

___(1994). Teachers' grading: Practice and Theory. *Applied Measurement in Education,* 7 (4), 279-301.

___(1993). Teachers' grading practices: Meaning and values. *Journal of Educational Measurement,* 30 (2), 123-142.

Brookhart, S. & Nitko, A. (2008). *Assessment and grading in classrooms.* Upper Saddle, NJ: Pearson.

Brooks, J. G. & Brooks, M. G. (1993). *In search of understanding: A case for constructivist classrooms.* Alexandria, VA: ASCD.

Butler, R. (1988). Enhancing and undermining intrinsic motivation: The effects of task-involving and ego-involving evaluation on interest and performance. *British Journal of Educational Psychology,* 58, 1-14.

Caine, R. N. & Caine, G. (1994). *Making connections: Teaching and the human brain.* New York, NY: Addison-Wesley.

Carr, J.F., & Harris, D.E. (2001). *Succeeding with standards.* Alexandria, VA: ASCD.

Colby, S. (1999). Grading in a standards-based system. *Educational Leadership,* 56 (6), 52-55.

Crooks, T.J. (1988). The impact of classroom evaluation practices on students. *Review of Educational Research,* 58, 438-481.

Delandshere, G. (2002). Assessment as inquiry [Electronic version]. *Teachers College Record,* 104 (7), 1461-1484.

Deutsch, M. (1979). Education and distributive justice: Some reflections on grading systems. *American Psychologist,* 34 (5), 391-401.

Doran, H.C. (2003). Adding value to accountability. *Educational Leadership,* 61 (3), 57.

DuFour, R. (2004). What is a "professional learning community?" *Educational Leadership,* 61 (8), 6-11.

Dunn, K., Scileppi, J., Averna, L., Zerillo, V., & Skelding, M. (2007). *The contemporary application of a systems approach to education: Models for effective reform.* (Chapter 3). Lanham, MD: University Press of America, Inc.

Dweck, C. (1992). Achievement goals and intrinsic motivation: Their relation and their role in adaptive motivation. *Motivation and Emotion,* 16 (3), 231-247.

Garet, M., Birman, B., Porter, A., Desimone, L., & Herman, B. (with Suk Yoon, K.). (1999). *Designing effective professional development: Lessons from the Eisenhower Program.* Washington, D.C.: U.S. Department of Education.

Glaser, R. (1981). The future of testing: A research agenda for cognitive psychology and psychometrics. *American Psychologist,* 36, 924.

Guskey, T. R. (1994). Making the grade: What benefits students? *Educational Leadership,* 52 (2): 14-20.

Herman, J. L., Aschbacher, P. R., & Winters, L. (1992). *A practical guide to alternative assessment.* Alexandria, VA: ASCD.

Illich, I. (1970). *Deschooling society.* New York, NY: Harper & Row.

Johnston, P. (1989). Constructive evaluation and improvement of teaching and learning. *Teachers College Record,* 90 (4), 509-528.

Kohn, A. (1996). *Punished by rewards.* New York, NY: Houghton-Mifflin.

___ (2000). *The case against standardized testing: Raising the scores, ruining the schools.* Westport, CT: Heinemann.

Langer, G.M., Colton, A.B., & Goff, L.S. (2003). *Collaborative analysis of student work: Improving teaching and learning.* Alexandria, VA: ASCD.

Lewin, L. & Shoemaker, B.J. (1998). *Great performances: Creating classroom-based assessment tasks.* Alexandria, VA: ASCD.

Marzano, R. J. (2006). *Classroom assessment & grading that work.* Alexandria, VA: ASCD.

___. (2000). *Transforming classroom grading.* Alexandria, VA: ASCD.

Marzano, R.J. & Kendall, J.S. (1996). *A comprehensive guide to designing standards-based districts, schools, and classrooms.* Alexandria, VA: ASCD.

Marzano, R.J., Pickering, D.J., &McTighe, J. (1993). *Assessing student outcomes: Performance assessment using the dimensions of learning model.* Alexandria, VA: ASCD.

Natriello, G. (1987). The impact of evaluation processes on students. *Educational Psychologist,* 22 (2), 155-175.

Noddings, N. (1992). *The challenge to care in schools.* New York, NY: Teachers College Press.

O'Connor, K. (2002). *How to grade for learning: Linking grades to standards.* Glenview, IL: Pearson Education, Inc.

O'Neill, K. & Stansbury, K. (2000). *Developing a standards-based assessment system.* San Francisco, CA: WestEd.

Popham, W.J. (2008). *Transformative assessment.* Alexandria, VA: ASCD.

___ (2003). *Test better, teach better: The instructional role of assessment.* Alexandria, VA: ASCD.

___ (2001). *The truth about testing: An educator's call to action.* Alexandria, VA: ASCD.

___ (1997). What's wrong – and what's right – with rubrics? *Educational Leadership*, 55 (2), 72-75.

Reeves, D. B. (2004). The case against the zero. *Phi Delta Kappan*, 86 (4): 324-325.

Schmoker, M. (1999). *Results: The key to continuous school improvement.* Alexandria, VA: ASCD.

Skelding, M. (2011). *Color blindness, phenomenology, and grading.* Education Week Online, February 11, 2011.

___ (2008). *Lasting results: Rediscovering the promise of standards through assessment-based instruction.* Montpelier, VT: Common Roots Press.

Stiggins, R. J. (2000). *Classroom assessment connections.* Portland, OR: Assessment Training Institute.

___ (1997). *Student-centered classroom assessment.* Upper Saddle, NJ: Prentice Hall.

Strong, R.W., Silver, H.F., & Perini, M.J. (2001(. *Teaching what matters most.* Alexandria, VA: ASCD.

Tomlinson, C.A. (2001). Grading for success. *Educational Leadership*, 3, 12-15.

Vermont Department of Education. (2004). *Grade expectations for Vermont's framework of standards and learning opportunities.* Montpelier, VT: Vermont Department of Education.

___ (2000). *Vermont framework of standards and learning opportunities.* Montpelier, VT: Vermont Department of Education.

___ (1996). *Core connections: A how-to-guide for using Vermont's framework.* Montpelier, VT: Vermont Department of Education.

Vygotsky, L. S. (1978). *Mind in society: The development of higher psychological processes.* Cambridge, MA: Harvard University Press.

Wadsworth, B. J. (1996). *Piaget's theory of cognitive and affective development.* White Plains, NY: Longman.

Whitney, D.T., Culligan, J.J., & Brooksher, P.T. (2006). *Truth in grading.* New York, NY: iUniverse, Inc.

Wiggins, G. (1998). *Educative assessment: Designing assessments to inform and improve performance.* San Francisco, CA: Jossey-Bass.

___ (1993). *Assessing student performance: Exploring the purpose and limits of testing.* San Francisco, CA: Jossey-Bass.

Wiggins, G. & McTighe, J. (1998). *Understanding by design.* Alexandria, VA: ASCD.

Wolfe, P. (2001). *Brain Matters: Translating Research into Classroom Practice.* Alexandria, VA: ASCD.

Wong, H.K. (2003). Collaborating with colleagues to improve student learning. *ENC Focus,* 11 (6). Retrieved July 8, 2004, from http://www.enc.org.

Wormeli, R. (2006). *Fair isn't always equal.* Portland, ME: Stenhouse

ACKNOWLEDGEMENTS

I gratefully acknowledge the following people for their role in making this book happen.

Robert Stanton, an exceptional education leader, a sincere advocate for students, a friend, and just a really good person. Thank you so much for giving me my start in public education.

Joseph Kiefer and Martin Kemple, two progressive sense of place and food security educators who genuinely care about social justice and sustainability. Thank you very much for my opportunity to enter the world of higher education.

Vanessa Zerillo, a friend, mentor, and courageous leader willing to risk pushing the norms of higher education. Thank you so much for my opportunity to work with so many Vermont educators and to be able to go as deep as I was able with my work on grading.

The hundreds of Vermont educators I had the great pleasure of getting to know and work with. Thank you for your assistance with this work.

Rachel Fisher, the Publishing Manager at Onion River Press. Thank you so much for making this book a reality.

Amy Tillotson, a super fun co-worker. Thanks for visually improving my "Trees Diagram."

And finally, progressive educators both past and present ... John Dewey, Jean Piaget, Jerome Bruner, Alfred North Whitehead, Ivan Illich, Nel Noddings, William Pinar, Chet Bowers, David Orr, and Grant Wiggins to name several. Thank you for helping me see public education for what it is ... and isn't.

ABOUT MARK SKELDING

After receiving his teaching degree from Michigan State University, Mark Skelding taught in a self-contained combined fifth and sixth grade classroom for five years at Fayston Elementary School in Fayston, Vermont. From there he went to Stowe Elementary and then Stowe Middle School in Stowe, Vermont where he team taught sixth grade science, social studies, and language arts for seven years.

He then left the classroom, earned his Master's Degree in Education from St. Michael's College in Colchester, Vermont, and became Ecological Literacy Director for Food Works/Two Rivers Center for Sustainability in Montpelier, Vermont. There he developed a graduate level Ecological Literacy/Schoolyard Habitat course which he taught to hundreds of teachers around the state of Vermont.

Six years later he became Academic Coordinator and Assistant Professor for Trinity College of Vermont's (Burlington, Vermont) and later Southern New Hampshire University's Vermont Center's Field-based Graduate Program in Education in Colchester, Vermont. There he developed and taught courses in formative assessment, evaluation, and action research. During his ten years at SNHU's Vermont Center he also conducted his study of the practice of grading students.

In addition to these classroom experiences he coached Little League baseball for ten seasons. He played organized baseball as well, from age eight playing second base for his Cub Scout team on up to Division III college ball. From eighth grade to the end of his career he played third base for both his school and summer ball teams. His idol is Hall of Fame third baseman Brooks Robinson and to this day he remains a loyal fan of the Baltimore Orioles and the Philadelphia Phillies.

He is the author of *Lasting Results: Rediscovering the Promise of Standards Through Assessment-based Instruction* (Common Roots Press, 2000), "*Color Blindness, Phenomenology, and Grading*" (Education Week online commentary, February 11, 2011), and co-author of *The Contemporary Application of a Systems Approach to Education: Models of Effective Reform* (University Press of America, 2007). He is also author of *Does Nature Approve? A Contemplation of Lawn Care Practices* (Onion River Press, 2020).

www.ingramcontent.com/pod-product-compliance
Lightning Source LLC
Chambersburg PA
CBHW022055020426
42335CB00012B/701